BUFFALO BILL
and the Wild West

HON. W. F. CODY
"BUFFALO BILL"

BUFFALO BILL
and the Wild West

THE BROOKLYN MUSEUM
MUSEUM OF ART, CARNEGIE INSTITUTE
BUFFALO BILL HISTORICAL CENTER

The exhibition sponsored by
Philip Morris Incorporated and
The Seven-Up Company

Distributed by the University of Pittsburgh Press

Contents

Buffalo Bill and the Wild West

Published for the exhibition
Buffalo Bill and the Wild West

The Brooklyn Museum, New York
November 21, 1981—January 17, 1982

Museum of Art, Carnegie Institute
Pittsburgh, Pennsylvania
February 13—April 4, 1982

This Exhibition is a joint project of The Brooklyn Museum; the Museum of Art, Carnegie Institute; and the Buffalo Bill Historical Center.
Sponsored by
Philip Morris Incorporated and The Seven-Up Company.

Frontispiece:
Henry Atwell Thomas
Portrait *circa* 1888
Poster
Printer: H. A. Thomas & Wylie Lithographers, New York
75.0 x 102.0 cm. (29 ½ x 40 in.)
Collection: Musée des Arts Décoratifs, Paris. From 100 Posters of Buffalo Bill's Wild West *by Jack Rennert, Copyright 1976 Darien House, Inc.*

Back Cover:
Irving R. Bacon
Detail from **Conquest of the Prairie**
1908
Oil on canvas
120.0 x 301.0 cm.
(47½ x 118½ in.)
Collection: Buffalo Bill Historical Center, Cody, Wyoming

Designed and published by The Brooklyn Museum, Division of Publications and Marketing Services, Eastern Parkway, Brooklyn, New York 11238.
Printed in the USA by the Falcon Press, Philadelphia.

© 1981 The Brooklyn Museum.

Library of Congress Cataloging in Publication Data
Main entry under title:

Buffalo Bill and the Wild West.

  Bibliography: p.
  Contents: Introduction/David Katzive—The Artists/Peter H. Hassrick—The Wild West/Richard Slotkin—[etc.]
  1. Bill, Buffalo, 1846—1917—Addresses, essays, lectures. 2. Pioneers—West (U.S.)—Biography—Addresses, essays, lectures.
3. West (U.S.)—Biography—Addresses, essays, lectures. I. Brooklyn Museum.
F594.C68B8   978'.02'0924   [B]   81—12198
ISBN 0—87273—082—4   AACR2

Buffalo Bill and the Wild West

Sponsor's Statement

George Weissman

*Chairman of the Board
and Chief Executive Officer
Philip Morris Incorporated*

Thundering hoof-beats out of the past herald the arrival once more of the cowboys and Indians, sharpshooters, scouts and Rough Riders of the breath-taking, spectacular and wondrous Wild West show, with the legendary Buffalo Bill—the incomparable frontiersman, showman, businessman and pioneer media star William Cody—right up front.

For today's generations, from the very young to those who can still remember back when, *Buffalo Bill and the Wild West* revives a great American show, perhaps the single most compelling show of our rambunctious history. It was an extravaganza without parallel that helped brand some of America's most vital characteristics—personal daring, vast territory, heroic achievements—into our common heritage; it thrilled and enchanted our nation, and created an enduring image of America abroad.

Philip Morris, mindful of frontier days and their special niche in our national culture, has occasionally travelled into the past and has gone west, in a landmark series of museum exhibitions, to offer new knowledge of our lavish history, and new insights into the shaping of our collective traits as a nation engaged in seemingly perpetual growth.

The legend of the frontier, personified by Buffalo Bill, still lives because it touches upon so many crucial phases of our evolution— from the anguish of the Civil War, up to, and even a bit beyond, World War I. Thanks to this panoramic exhibition, its publication and related programs and events, we now possess keener understanding of that period of enormous change, and of its impact upon our traditions and national character.

The presentation of circumstances, events and individuals in dynamic interaction often helps to restore legends—facing oblivion through waning purpose, neglect and fading memory—to robust life. It achieves this by rooting legends in fact and investing them with more precise, more permanent definition. The refurbished legends help to tell us who we were in the process of becoming who we are.

Buffalo Bill and the Wild West will not only appear in Brooklyn and Pittsburgh but also march through almost every city, town and hamlet in the country as part of Macy's televised Thanksgiving Day Parade. There will be eighty million spectators on the sidelines cheering the colorful contingent, gleefully shouting their approval of this recreation of Bill Cody's Wild West show.

And in the lead, where it belongs, will be the spirit of Buffalo Bill himself atop his proud ghost horse—measuring the scope of our progress since his last earthly appearance more than sixty years ago, accepting the changes he sees without breaking stride, and, of course, at the same time, counting the house. All this is part and parcel of the legend and the reality of William Cody, one of the most remarkable and memorable of all American figures.

His returning presence reminds us that the American frontier was no mere legend. It did exist, with its towering mountain ranges and endless plains, and it helped to forge the American temper. Long after it was officially marked "closed," the frontier remained open in our consciousness: "the bountiful infinite West," that vast nursing ground of our irrepressible individualism, boundless energy, hardy spirit and unflagging optimism.

We need that frontier, extending from the Atlantic to the Pacific—and into space. For where it exists, there will always be open, inquisitive, daring minds. So long as we remain free to roam for new worlds to conquer—be they in the sciences, art, material progress or human betterment—there will always be a Wild West show, with Buffalo Bill at the head, in the arena of America's shared national imagination.

Buffalo Bill and the Wild West

Foreword

Michael Botwinick

Director
The Brooklyn Museum, New York

John R. Lane

Director
Museum of Art, Carnegie Institute
Pittsburgh, Pennsylvania

Just before the American Bicentennial we became enthusiastic about the idea of an exhibition that would focus on some aspect of the American West. That project was never realized. But we did not lose our enthusiasm for such a show.

One of the institutions that we had hoped to draw on for loans was the Buffalo Bill Historical Center in Cody, Wyoming. As the Bicentennial project faded, the possibilities presented by the Center's collections became clearer. Now consisting of four major areas—The Whitney Gallery of Western Art, The Plains Indian Museum, The Winchester Museum and The Buffalo Bill Museum—the Center sits on the plains of the Rockies, near Yellowstone National Park, in the city that Buffalo Bill himself founded. Each year, during the severe winter months, there is a kind of hibernation. While research and collection study goes on, few members of the visiting public make the journey. We proposed that the Buffalo Bill Historical Center have a kind of winter season; that some of the collections be organized into an an exhibition that could tour when there was no real public attendence at Cody.

Peter Kriendler, a Buffalo Bill Historical Center trustee was an early and staunch supporter of this notion. He recognized that it would allow many more people to see some of the special quality of the Buffalo Bill Historical Center collection. He has been a mainstay of the project to its fruition, and we are all grateful to him.

Under the able and vigorous leadership of Director Peter Hassrick, and with the encouragement of Chairman of the Board Mrs. Henry H. R. Coe, the Center has taken an active and important role in the shaping of this project. The Center's collection is a very special one, and neither the

exhibition nor this handsome publication do it thorough justice. But thanks to Dr. Hassrick and his staff, we hope they convey some sense of the vision that is the West. Gene Ball, Paul Fees, Richard Frost and George Horsecapture, all of the Buffalo Bill Historical Center staff were extremely helpful at every stage of the undertaking. We are also grateful to Royal Hassrick, Richard Pohrt and Miles Liphardt, consultants to the Buffalo Bill Historical Center, for their advice, and to Bill Cody and Fred Garlow, Buffalo Bill's grandsons, for their generous sharing of history and memory.

We are especially grateful to the authors of the essays that follow. Each, in pursuing his own course, has given us a unique and provocative image of Buffalo Bill. We would like to thank Walter Menninger for his helpfulness and patience. We are extremely grateful to Robert Venables, Curator of American Indian History at the Museum of the American Indian, Heye Foundation, for his assistance in compiling the chronology of events, and to Linda Ferber and Diana Fane of The Brooklyn Museum for their assistance.

Realizing so ambitious an undertaking over long distances has not been easy, and was only made possible by the contributions of many people. We are indebted to Elaine Loring and Robert Baron of The Brooklyn Museum for their work on the initial research and planning, to Emily Beck, who accomplished the task of editing the essays with much grace, and to Lise Michelman, coordinator of the exhibition, for stepping in and handling so many of the details. David Katzive, Director of the DeCordova and Dana Museum, Lincoln, Massachusetts, who was Assistant Director at The Brooklyn Museum at the beginning of the

project, could not part himself from *Buffalo Bill and the Wild West.* An how lucky we all were. That the project came through is as much a product of his vigor and dedicatio as it is a testimony to his lively intellect and willingness to stretch boundries of what we all think we can do.

Our sponsor, Philip Morris Incorporated, has a distinguished tradition of supporting exhibitions the past this corporation has been the critical element in making it possible for museums both in the United States and abroad to prese exhibitions dealing not only with t West, but also with folk art, black artists and women, to mention bu few. The supportive role that Phil Morris has adopted gives us all a chance to look back over our shoulders and learn something about where we come from. We salute all of the people of Philip Morris Incorporated and The Seven-Up Company for their support.

We don't know whether *Buffalo B and the Wild West* separates myth from reality. But the story of the coming of age of America in the nineteenth century—and that, aft all, is so much of what Buffalo Bill about—is as much a matter of my as it is a matter of historical fact. W have fueled ourselves for generations on the rich legend of Buffalo Bill. And to the extent that this legend teaches us about courage, loyalty, independence, self-reliance, perseverance and the simple sheer delight at the majesty this land, we should cherish it.

The Wild West show on parade
Courtesy The Denver Public Library,
Western History Department, Colorado

Buffalo Bill and the Wild West

Introduction

David H. Katzive

Director
DeCordova and Dana Museum
and Park
Lincoln, Massachusetts

In developing *Buffalo Bill and the Wild West*, we had many occasions to ask people if they had ever heard of Buffalo Bill and what they knew about him. The responses, from both the general and well-educated public, were surprisingly similar. People would immediately recognize the name but then add inaccurate details, often confusing Buffalo Bill with Wild Bill Hickok and defining him as a cowboy, gunfighter, bandit or, occasionally, circus star. All of the usual stereotypes of the cowboys and Indians were evoked by the name of Buffalo Bill, but the mere mention of a few facts, particularly his association with Annie Oakley, triggered a set of memories that at least placed Buffalo Bill in a more accurate context—as frontiersman, scout, showman, entrepreneur. This perception of his life appeared to lie just below the level of popular

Right:
Poster
Portrait 1908
Printer: Strobridge Lithographic Co., Cincinnati, Ohio
2-sheet: 147 x 102 cm. (58 x 40 in.)
Collection: Buffalo Bill Historical Center, Cody, Wyoming

Below:
Poster
Marksmanship—Foot and Horseback 1898
Printer: Enquirer Job Printing Co., Cincinnati, Ohio
9-sheet: 212 x 316 cm. (83 x 123½ in.)
Collection: Circus World Museum of Baraboo, Wisconsin

Left:
William F. Cody at age 14 (top), and at 22 (center)
Courtesy Buffalo Bill Historical Center, Cody, Wyoming

Right, top:
Cody with his wife, Louisa, and his daughters Arta (standing) and Irma (center), St. Louis, *circa* 1889
Courtesy Buffalo Bill Historical Center, Cody, Wyoming

Right, bottom:
Buffalo Bill in fur coat and pin-striped suit, New York, *circa* 1875
Courtesy Buffalo Bill Historical Center, Cody, Wyoming

Below:
Cody's boyhood home in LeClaire, Iowa
Courtesy Buffalo Bill Historical Center, Cody, Wyoming

knowledge enriched with cowboys, Indians and gunplay that the average American carries as part of our national folklore.

The intertwining of myth and actuality was a very real aspect of the life of William F. "Buffalo Bill" Cody from the late 1860s until his death in 1917. He was America's first media hero—initially in popular literature and on stage and then, to a lesser degree, in films and commercial endorsements. Scholarship on Cody abounds with phrases like "myth vs. reality," "life vs. legend," "fact vs. fiction." Understandably, these terms occur with great frequency in the essays that follow.

A related problem, which we encountered at the beginning of our research, is the enormity of information and images concerning Buffalo Bill, his times and his milieu. With over a billion words published about him before the turn of the century, he ranks as one of the most famous characters in American history, rivaling Thomas Jefferson, George Washington or Abraham Lincoln.

Contrary to the superficial impressions of the public, Cody was not a gunfighter or a cowboy; he was a skilled hunter, scout and showman. If the average American thinks of guns, horses, cowboys and Indians at the mention of the frontier, there can be little doubt that Cody's enterprises served as a primary source for such stereotypes. It is the flavor, the noise and color, rather than the content of the Wild West show that Hollywood filmmakers most frequently captured. What is often unrecognized is the breadth and ambition of Cody's business enterprises. It is well-documented that he built hotels, founded a town, effected the construction of a railroad line, vigorously promoted land irrigation projects, ran a

Above:
Cody, Wyoming, 1905
Courtesy Buffalo Bill Historical Center, Cody, Wyoming

Right:
The Buffalo Bill Dam and Canyon, two miles west of Cody, Wyoming, *circa* 1959
Courtesy Buffalo Bill Historical Center, Cody, Wyoming

Below:
An advertisement for the Cody Canal, from the newspaper *The Cody Enterprise,* September 28, 1899.
Collection: Buffalo Bill Historical Center, Cody, Wyoming

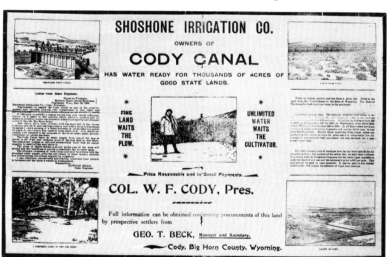

Far Left:
Cover for sheet music
Collection: Buffalo Bill Historical Center, Cody, Wyoming

Left:
Cody relaxes in the doorway of his tent, behind the scenes at the Wild West, *circa* 1900.
Courtesy Buffalo Bill Historical Center, Cody, Wyoming

multi-million dollar business operation in the form of the Wild West show, made films, served as the head of the Showman's League of America—and then, toward the end of his life, lost control of his business affairs and became a victim of unscrupulous dealings and opportunistic business interests.

Accordingly, we commissioned a set of interpretive essays on six specific themes suggested by the complex career of William F. Cody. At the heart of them is Don Russell's *Lives and Legends of Buffalo Bill.* This book serves as the basic reference tool for any author or scholar, balancing conflicting accounts and including an impressive bibliography, with many primary source references.

To accompany the essays, we have created a chronology of the major events of Cody's life, set against the larger context of important dates in the history of this period. The essays themselves represent the opinions and research of art historian Peter Hassrick; a specialist in American history, Howard Lamar; an expert in political science and the history of Native Americans, Vine Deloria, Jr.; two professors of English and scholars in the history of American literature, Leslie Fiedler and Richard

Above:
Poster
Portrait *circa* 1898
Printer: Enquirer Job Printing Co., Cincinnati, Ohio
12-sheet: 279 x 316 cm. (109 x 123½ in.)
Collection: Circus World Museum of Baraboo, Wisconsin

Right:
The image of Buffalo Bill used as an endorsement
Courtesy The Denver Public Library, Western History Department, Colorado

Far right:
Cody's enlistment papers for the 7th Kansas Volunteer Cavalry, known as Jennison's Jayhawkers, dated February 17, 1864

Slotkin; and a specialist in the history of film, William Judson.

As this collection of articles demonstrates, the forces that motivated Cody's career are complex and elusive. The essays that present the most complete sense of Cody's personality are those of Vine Deloria and Leslie Fiedler. In a manner indicative of the opposing views of Cody, they are in curious conflict with one another; one author seeks to discover acts of faith and noble character, while the other sees, in the same historic incidents, droll hypocrisy and irony.

Left:
Buffalo Bill with children at the Wild West show
Courtesy New York Public Library Picture Collection

Below:
The Buffalo Bill Historical Center in Cody, Wyoming
Courtesy Buffalo Bill Historical Center, Cody, Wyoming

Bottom:
Buffalo Bill in the saddle
Courtesy Buffalo Bill Historical Center, Cody, Wyoming

A specific instance of this occurs with the 1876 Battle of War Bonnet Creek, in which Cody is purported to have scalped the Cheyenne warrior Yellow Hand, though whether he actually killed him is not proven. Deloria cites the incident as an illustration of Cody's admirable ability to attract publicity to himself, and uses it as the basis for a discussion of his bravery, scouting ability and marksmanship. Fiedler and Slotkin discuss this same event, accepting Cody's heroic role—as described by newspaper reports at the time—and focusing instead on the interpenetration of theater and reality represented by the occurrence. The tone of Fiedler's essay suggests that in general, Cody performed multiple roles somewhat innocently, driven by subjective needs and circumstances of fate into the presentation of himself as a hero. Slotkin attributes more cunning and calculation to Cody, going on to suggest that the entire Wild West enterprise was an elaborate reflection of a sensitivity to national concerns.

The most important aspect of this publication is that it is primarily

about Buffalo Bill. We are not attempting to tell the story of the Plains Indian, the buffalo or the complex phenomenon of the American frontier. The essays are focused on the issue of romanticizir the frontier—on mythmaking—an the degree to which this process ha shaped the American spirit and popular culture.

This issue is uniquely embodied in the life of William F. Cody. By becoming his own biographer, historian and educator, Cody adde an extraordinary dimension to his personal achievements, converting himself into a living historic artifact. In the programs for the Wild West show, he proclaimed himself to be an "authentic participant, repeating heroic parts played in actual life . . . Upon the plains, in the wilderness, mountain fastness and in the dread and dangerous scenes of savage an cruel warfare . . . in an exhibition . . . through the medium of animated pictures, in the picturesqu life on the Western American Plains in the days just past . . .", fueling what Leslie Fiedler describes as "th legend that refuses to die."

Left, top:
Buffalo Bill reenacting the scalping of the Cheyenne leader Yellow Hand for his 1913 film *The Indian Wars*
Courtesy Buffalo Bill Memorial Museum, Golden, Colorado

Left, center:
Robert Lindneux
Detail from **First Scalp for Custer** 1928
Oil on canvas
182.9 x 426.8 cm. (72 x 168 in.)
Collection: Buffalo Bill Historical Center, Cody, Wyoming

Left, bottom;
Paul Newman as Buffalo Bill in Robert Altman's *Buffalo Bill and the Indians, or Sitting Bull's History Lesson,* 1976
Collection: The Museum of Modern Art, Film Stills Archive, New York
Courtesy United Artists Corporation

Above:
The last photograph of Cody at his T.E.
Ranch on the south fork of the Shoshone
River, Wyoming, 1916
*Courtesy Buffalo Bill Historical Center,
Cody, Wyoming*

Left:
Post of a stair stoop 1900—1910
Brownstone; 40.6 x 40.6 x 7.6 cm.
(16 x 16 x 3 in.)
Original location: The Bronx, New York
*Collection: The Brooklyn Museum, New
York. Gift of White & Kaufman through
the Anonymous Art Recovery Society*
65.115.3-9

Right:
"Gone to Join the Mysterious Caravan,"
a cartoon commentary on Buffalo Bill's
death
*Collection: Buffalo Bill Historical Center,
Cody, Wyoming*

BOYHOOD'S GREAT IDOL

Chronology of Events

1804—05 Lewis and Clark cross the continent to chart the Louisiana Purchase of 1803.

1830 Congress, at the request of President Andrew Jackson, passes the Indian Removal Act, forcing ninety-two percent of all the Indians living east of the Mississippi to the West.

1830—32 Artist George Catlin (1796—1872) makes three trips to the West; visits at least seventeen Indian nations.

1837 Artist Alfred Jacob Miller (1810—1874) makes his first trip to the West.

1849 Thousands of Easterners illegally cross Indian Territory in the rush for California gold.

1851 Treaty signed at Fort Laramie, Wyoming; U.S. gets permission from the Indians to build roads and forts in Indian Territory in exchange for annuities.

1854 Russell, Majors and Waddell organize leading Western freighting company.

1859 Artist Albert Bierstadt (1830—1902) visits the Shoshones and the Sioux (also known as the Lakotas).

1860 Russell and Majors organize the Pony Express using riders whose average age is 19. It lasts only a year, made obsolete by the first transcontinental telegraph line.

1861—65 Civil War

1862 Congress passes the Homestead and Pacific Railroad acts, grants of Indian land to whites, in order to clear the way for a transcontinental railroad.

1864 Dozens of Cheyenne and Arapaho families, living in peace under U.S. government protection, are slaughtered by Colonel John Chivington at Sand Creek in eastern Colorado.

1868 The second Fort Laramie treaty creates the Great Sioux Reservation; the Sioux are guaranteed their sacred land, the Black Hills, and retain the right to hunt in the Powder River region.

1868—69 The transcontinental railroad is completed.

1869 Battle of Summit Springs: 5th Cavalry defeats the Cheyennes led by Tall Bull in Colorado, insuring continued white expansion onto Indian lands.

1871 Introduction of commercial tanning makes buffalo hide useful for fine leather products.

1874 Introduction of barbed wire signals beginning of the end of open-range cattle grazing.
Treaty with the Sioux violated: George Custer leads a major expedition into the Black Hills and finds gold.

1876 The Sioux, under their spiritual leader Sitting Bull, and the Cheyennes, under Two Moon, defeat Custer and his troops at the Battle of the Little Big Horn, Montana—Custer's Last Stand.
The Cheyenne leader, Yellow Hand, is killed at the Battle of War Bonnet Creek, a minor battle in the aftermath of Custer's death.

1877 Sitting Bull and his Sioux followers take refuge in Canada.

WILLIAM F. "BUFFALO BILL" CODY

1846 Born February 26, near LeClaire, Iowa.

1857—59 Hired as a messenger for Majors and Russell Co. in Kansas; serves on wagon trains and cattle drives, and makes his first trip across the Plains.

1860 Rides for the Pony Express; at the age of 15 makes the third longest trip of 322 miles. Later, the Pony Express gains notoriety and is featured as an act in the Wild West show.

1864 Enlists in the 7th Kansas Volunteer Cavalry, known as Jennison's Jayhawkers.

1864 Enlists in the 7th Kansas Volunteer Cavalry, known as Jennison's Jayhawkers.

1865 Works as a scout and dispatch bearer for General William Tecumseh Sherman in Kansas.

1866 Marries Louisa Frederici.

1867—68 Acquires the name Buffalo Bill while under contract to provide buffalo meat for the workers of the Kansas Pacific Railroad. "During my engagement as hunter for the company," he later writes, "I killed 4,280 buffaloes."

1868—72 Employed as a scout and guide for the U.S. Cavalry, most notably as chief of scouts for the 5th Cavalry.

1869 *Buffalo Bill, the King of Border Men,* written by Ned Buntline, is published—the first of more than 550 different dime novels about Buffalo Bill.

1872 Guides buffalo hunting party and provides "Indian" entertainment for Grand Duke Alexis of Russia. Begins eleven-season stage career by playing himself in a melodrama of frontier life.

1873 Forms the "Buffalo Bill Combination," a traveling theatrical troupe, with Wild Bill Hickok and Texas Jack Omohundro; confines his scouting to the summer months.

1876 Produces and stars in *The Red Right Hand; or, Buffalo Bill's First Scalp for Custer,* a dramatization of the War Bonnet battle.

1878   Indian-manned police forces, are established by the U.S. government for reservation supervision.
The southern herd of buffalo nears extinction.

1880   The Northern Pacific Railroad is completed.

1881   Artist Frederic Remington (1861—1909) makes his first trip to the West.
A Century of Dishonor, an indictment of U.S. Indian policy by Helen Hunt Jackson, is published.
Sitting Bull returns to the U.S. from Canada; the Army breaks its promise of a pardon and holds him as a military prisoner.

1883   Sitting Bull participates in the last traditional buffalo hunt of the Sioux; the northern herd is now virtually extinct.

1887   Congress passes the Dawes Allotment Act, dividing reservation lands on a basis of 160 acres per head of family. The stated intent is to make Indians private-property owners and end their preference for communally-held land. But it also takes away "excess" Indian lands, and results in the loss of more than three quarters of the remaining Indian land.

1889   Ignoring Sitting Bull's advice, the Sioux agree to sell the U.S. nine million acres, carving the Great Sioux Reservation into six smaller reservations.
Six hundred thirty-five buffalo are reported running wild in all of North America.

1890   The Ghost Dance, a religious movement which originated with the Paiute prophet Wovoka, reaches the Sioux. It promises the disappearance of the white man and the return of the buffalo. On December 15, Sitting Bull is shot and killed by Indian police attempting to arrest him. On December 29, more than three hundred Sioux are massacred at Wounded Knee by the 7th Cavalry.
The Census Bureau reports continous settlement across the continent: "The unsettled area has been so broken into by isolated bodies of settlement that there can hardly be said to be a frontier line."

1898   Spanish-American War breaks out; Teddy Roosevelt leads his Rough Riders at the Battle of San Juan Hill.

1901   Roosevelt becomes President after the assassination of William McKinley.

1917   The United States enters World War I.

1878   Uses reservation Indians as actors in stage melodramas for the first time.

1879   Publishes *The Life of Hon. William F. Cody, Known as Buffalo Bill, the Famous Hunter, Scout and Guide: An Autobiography.*

1882   Organizes an "Old Glory Blowout," a Fourth of July celebration in North Platte, Nebraska—a precursor to the Wild West show.

1883   Presents first Wild West show in Omaha, Nebraska—sometimes billed as "The Wild West, Hon. W. F. Cody and Dr. W. F. Carver's Rocky Mountain and Prairie Exhibition."

1884   Annie Oakley joins the show as "Little Sure Shot," except for 1888, she remains with the Wild West until 1901.

1885—86   Sitting Bull joins the show for a season.

1887   The Wild West show is part of the American exhibition at Queen Victoria's Jubilee in London. The show regularly tours Europe until 1906.
Given the title of Colonel by the governor of Nebraska.

1893   Wild West show opens next to the World's Columbian Exposition in Chicago; the act "Congress of Rough Riders of the World" is introduced.

1895—96   Develops town of Cody, Wyoming.

1899   Sixteen of Roosevelt's Rough Riders join the Wild West and participate in a dramatization of the taking of San Juan Hill.

1902   Forms the Cody-Dyer Mining and Milling Company; loses much of his Wild West profits in this unsuccessful venture.

1905   Sues his wife for divorce.

1907   Portrays himself as Tall Bull's killer in a Wild West reenactment of the Battle of Summit Springs.

1908   Wild West merges with Pawnee Bill's Great Far East.

1910   Begins series of farewell appearances.

1913   The Col. W. F. Cody (Buffalo Bill) Historical Pictures Company is formed to produce short films on the Indian wars.

1914—15   Travels with the Sells-Floto circus.

1916   Joins and makes his final appearance with Miller Brothers and Arlington 101 Ranch Wild West; theme of the show is military preparedness.

1917   Dies January 10 in Denver, Colorado, and is buried on Lookout Mountain.

Buffalo Bill and the Wild West

The Artists

Peter H. Hassrick

Director
Buffalo Bill Historical Center
Cody, Wyoming

The life of William F. Cody can be divided into two distinct phases. Until he reached his mid-thirties he was primarily engaged in the work of the frontier and the theater, serving as a wagon driver, Pony Express rider, hunter, scout and guide. On stage he performed for nearly a dozen years in melodramas set in the same Plains environment where he had worked as a real character during this often romanticized chapter of American history.

In the second half of his life, Cody consciously assumed the role of an educator and showman, seeking to preserve and share what he perceived as a vanishing saga of history and heroism on the frontier. He also had the sense to hire good businessmen and specialists in what would come to be called public relations. They helped him to develop and promote his extravagant "object lessons" for an Eastern and foreign audience eager to see and hear tales of the West. Cody's career paralleled those of such artists as George Catlin and Albert Bierstadt, who exhibited their work in special salons and charged admission to the throngs of visitors who came to marvel at the grandeur or mystery of the exotic West. Cody also established relationships with Remington, Russell, Schreyvogel and others—as discussed here by Peter Hassrick. Cody's interest in Western art is consistent with his impulse to convey images to vast audiences as either a showman, filmaker, or author. Those paintings that he commissioned furthered the cause of documenting Western legends, and usually featured Buffalo Bill as the the main character. [DHK]

The Tower, the Parliament, and Westminster are older institutions in London than Buffalo Bill's show, but when the New-Zealander sits on the London Bridge and looks over his . . . Murray's Guide-book, he is going to turn first to the Wild West.

Frederic Remington (London, 1892)[1]

Frederic Remington was one of many artists who recognized the unique synthesis of legend and fac drama and history that preserved spirit of America's Far West in Buffalo Bill's shows. An artist who devoted his own career to this san aggregation of elements, Remingt knew what stirred the senses of those who enjoyed Cody's extravaganzas from the benches o the Wild West show arena. He cou appreciate the universal appeal of the Western image—how it struck harmonious chord in the hearts of Americans and Europeans alike.

And, as he strove in his paintings and bronzes to interpret and portray the Western saga, he also enjoyed speculating on the impact of those like Buffalo Bill who lived to glorify its image in live performance.

On his way home from an abortive junket to Russia in the fall of 1892, Remington found solace in the sight of Cody's tents set curiously on the lawn of Earl's Court in London. Here was not simply a touch of home, but the promise of history preserved. As he wrote to *Harper's Weekly,* "One should no longer ride the deserts of Texas or the rugged uplands of Wyoming to see the Indians and the pioneers, but should go to London."[2]

Here too was promise of a continuing tradition, one as old as the nineteenth century was long—one devoted to recording, exploiting and popularizing the symbols of the past. When Remington wrote that "The Wild West show is an evolution of a great idea,"[3] he was not referring merely to its circus elements as developed by such precursors as P.T. Barnum. He saw the Wild West show as an extension of such fundamental frontier traits as individualism and self-reliance. In Remington's vision, it represented "a poetical and harmless protest against the Derby hat and the starched linen—those horrible badges of the slavery of our modern social system, when men are physical lay figures, and mental and moral cog-wheels and works of uniformity—where the greatest crime is to be individual, and the unpardonable sin to be out of fashion."[4]

Frederic Remington and William F. Cody were companions both in the sense of their common goal and by personal acquaintance. They never, so far as the record stands, cooperated on any projects, yet they shared a time and a cause which allied their focus, their output and

Facing page, center:
Remington sketches of cossack and gaucho performers in the Wild West show in London, from *Harper's Weekly,* September 3, 1892

Facing page, bottom:
Frederic Remington (1861—1909)
Courtesy Remington Art Museum, Ogdensburg, New York

Left:
Poster
Horticultural Exhibition 1892
Printer: Stafford & Co., Netherfield, England
51 x 76 cm. (20 x 30 in.)
Courtesy Don Russell, Elmhurst, Illinois

Below:
Poster
Napoleon, Bonheur & Buffalo Bill 1898
Printer: Courier Lithographic Co., Buffalo, New York
67 x 100 cm. (26½ x 39in.)
Collection: Library of Congress, Washington, D.C.

their audience. Such a union of forces, of artistry and showmanship was not new, and it was to this poir also that Remington alluded when he spoke of an evolving tradition.

The wedding of extravaganza and art has never been foreign to American sensibilities. The nation's first museum, opened in 1786 and operated for the public benefit by the illustrious Peale family of Philadelphia, sold tickets on which vistor would read, ''The Birds and Beasts will teach thee! Admit the Bearer to Peale's Museum, containing the Wonderful Works of Nature and Curious Works of Art.'' A testament to the interrelation of art, science and history, Peale's Museum played to the fancy of an enthusiastic audience that saw in these combined disciplines something greater than its own experience could engender.

In the mid-1780s Charles Willson Peale, the museum's first director, was responsible for designing a ''landscape show-box,'' a device offering a rotating series of painting that depicted military engagements and exotic scenery.[6] About the sam time, an Englishman named Rober Baker introduced to Europe the Panorama, an enormous, circular version of the show-box. When the idea caught on in America, one of the first major productions planned was a dramatic display of what was then very much a frontier scene: a panoramic view of Niagara Falls by John Trumbull. Only the sketches remain today, yet the magnitude of Trumbull's vision in exploring such romantic scenery aptly illustrated th early potential for combining the enterprises of showmanship and fin art.[7]

Of the early artists who explored th Far West, George Catlin served bes to promote a public awareness and to achieve a common expression for art, science and showmanship. His adventures in the West had begun i

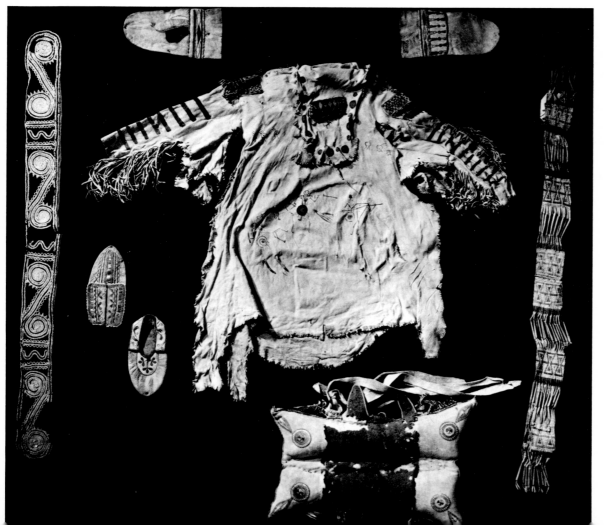

1830 and resulted in what was initially referred to as Catlin's *Gallery Unique.* In spirit his exhibition was modeled after Peale's Museum, with paintings augmented and, in fact, brought to life by a vast assemblage of Indian paraphernalia. A Crow tipi, Commanche lances, fringed scalp shirts, shields, headdresses, painted robes and an extraordinary array of other artifacts were included among the portraits and scenes of Indian life. Of the Crow tipi Catlin was most ebullient. He boasted of it as a "very splendid thing, brought from the foot of the Rocky Mountains, twenty-five feet in height, made of Buffalo skins, garnished and painted . . . ."[8]

By 1837, his materials fully amassed, the artist opened his exhibition as *Catlin's Indian Gallery* at Clinton Hall in New York City.

Top:
George Catlin
Crow Chief n.d.
Oil on board
43.8 x 58.7 cm. (17¼ x 23⅛ in.)
Collection: Buffalo Bill Historical Center,
Cody, Wyoming

Above, left:
George Catlin
Buffalo Hunt: The Surround n.d.
Handcolored lithograph
30.5 x 44. 8 cm. (12 x 17⅝ in.)
Collection: Buffalo Bill Historical Center,
Cody, Wyoming

Above, right:
Catlin painting a Mandan chief

Left:
Gertrude Vanderbilt Whitney
The Scout 1923
Bronze
Height: 378.5 cm. (149 in.)
Collection: Buffalo Bill Historical Center,
Cody, Wyoming

The New York *Morning Herald* for October 3 advised its readers that the artist had gotten very much in the spirit of things. "Mr. Catlin dressed himself in the attire of a Crow Indian. There is no modern civilized raiment that we have ever seen that can compare with it for beauty." The next day, Catlin's advertisement in the same newspaper suggested that costume was not the only theatrical ploy to be considered. "In order to render the exhibition more instructive than it could otherwise be, the paintings will be exhibited one at a time, and such explanation of their dress, customs, traditions, given by Mr. Catlin, as will enable the public to form a just idea of the customs, numbers, and condition of the savages yet in a state of nature in North America." As one Catlin biographer has noted, "It was the first *Wild West* show. It was a rip-roaring success.[9]

Two years later the artist sailed for Europe. His baggage contained eight tons of Western materials. By this time he even had a pair of grizzly bears in his company, thus animating the scene if not somewhat complicating affairs. Opening at London's Egyptian Hall in early 1840, he was immediately a popular sensation.

To maintain the vitality of his show and to spice up his lectures, Catlin

Above:
Alfred Jacob Miller
Trappers Saluting the Rocky Mountains n.d.
Oil on canvas
63.5 x 98.7 cm. (25 x 38⅞ in.)
Collection: Buffalo Bill Historical Center, Cody, Wyoming

Right:
Alfred Jacob Miller
Approaching Buffalo n.d.
Watercolor
19.4 x 32.7 cm. (7⅝ x 12⅞ in.)
Collection: Buffalo Bill Historical Center, Cody, Wyoming

Below, right:
Alfred Jacob Miller
Our Camp n.d.
Oil on canvas
67.0 x 91.4 cm. (26⅜ x 36 in.)
Collection: Buffalo Bill Historical Center, Cody, Wyoming

Facing page:
John Mix Stanley
Last of Their Race 1857
Oil on canvas
109.2 x 152.4 cm. (43 x 60 in.)
Collection: Buffalo Bill Historical Center, Cody, Wyoming

introduced in England what he called *tableaux vivants*—live reenactments of some of the stirring Indian scenes he had witnessed. At first he was forced to employ local actors; later he was able to supply real Indians. With a troupe of Ojibway performers he entertained young Queen Victoria. Some forty years later Buffalo Bill would perform similarly, but on a much grander scale, for the Queen's Golden Jubilee.

Such renown did Catlin achieve with his Indian expeditions that he continued and expanded the practice after moving to Paris in 1845. Ultimately, however, art and extravaganza did not mix well for Catlin. His Indian actors provided mostly headaches, many died of illness, others walked off the job homesick. His wife, Sara, admonished that he was not a showman but a painter. His declining fortunes and successes proved that perhaps she was right.[10]

☐   ☐

Back in 1837, while Catlin was playing to the curious social set of Manhattan, a young Baltimore artist named Alfred Jacob Miller avidly painted a scene to be preserved for posterity by him and him alone. This was the West's first genuine,

home-grown Wild West show, held at the foot of the Rocky Mountains. In the retinue of the Scottish nobleman William Drummond Stewart, Miller was brought west to provide pictorial analogue to the distant and exotic mountain man era. The highlight of his trip to the Wind River Mountains of present-day Wyoming was in observing the celebrated annual rendezvous of the fur trappers and Indians. Miller recounted in his notes that, "The first day is devoted to 'High Jinks', a species of Saturnalia, in which feasting, drinking, and gambling form prominent parts."[11] Six years later, Mathew Field, an observer at a subsequent affair of this sort, summarized his impressions: "300 whites—3 Indian villages—Nepercys, Flatheads and Snakes—1500 lodges Ec. The month of August—drinking—gaming, racing, singing, dancing, fighting, hunting, trading, fanfaronading, fishing, intriguing Ec. Ec. Ec."[12] Here audience and participant were one, and the diverse human elements represented a mixture of aspirations for these Western men—to collide in social intercourse, to bargain for gain or loss, and to disperse again into the selfness afforded only by the promise of a vast, uninhabited domain. This promise was shared too by those who viewed Catlin's

performances, though the wilderness was at once distant and vicarious.

Catlin and Miller met several times in London when Miller returned with his patron to paint a series of Far West showpieces for the walls of Stewart's Scottish castle. Miller felt there was a certain amount of humbug about his compatriot but then their approaches had been very different. Catlin had brought the Wild West to the doorsteps of Europe's nobility, while Miller had escorted nobility into the Wild West itself.

Many other artists of the period gleaned inspiration from the Far West and particularly from the Indian, as a symbol of that wilderness region. Seth Eastman, James Otto Lewis, Charles Bird King, John Mix Stanley and others assembled galleries of Indian portraits and scenes that met with varying degrees of popular success. Of these, Stanley was probably most renowned. By 1850 his *Stanley's North American Indian Gallery* was advertised as

> containing 134 Oil Paintings consisting of Portraits, Life size of the principal Chiefs and Warriors of fifty different tribes roving upon our Western and South-Western Prairies, New-Mexico, California and Oregon, together with

Landscape views, Games, Dances, Buffalo Hunts and Domestic Scenes, all of which have been painted in their own country during eight years travel among them, the whole forming one of the most interesting and instructive exhibitions illustrative of Indian life and customs ever before presented to the public.[13]

As with Catlin's production, people turned out also to see live Indians in Stanley's show. For example, George Copway, an Ojibway luminary, discoursed on "The Religious Belief, Poetry and Eloquence of the North American Indians." All who attended were, as the record indicates, "much pleased with the entertainment."[14]

By 1852 Stanley's gallery had moved to Washington, D.C., where, under a new title, *Portraits of North American Indians,* it was soon deposited with the Smithsonian Institution. "Our citizens can scarcely spend an hour more pleasantly than in a visit to these interesting pictures,"[15] wrote the *National Intelligencer.*

Though such a collection rivaled even Catlin's production, Stanley's exhibition still lacked vitality in the public's opinion. To remedy the situation, the artist embarked on the design of a huge moving panorama appropriately titled *Western Wilds.* Completed late in 1854, it was first displayed at the National Theater. "Unlike most other panoramas," observed a Washington paper, "this will bear frequent looking at. The scenes were all carefully painted on the spot, by an artist eminent in such representations. Members of Congress will be interested, as the panorama shows the nature of the country through which the Northern Railroad route to the Pacific is destined to pass."[16] With Stanley narrating as the great canvas unrolled, viewers were visually

escorted across the continent—"Over the mountain, the prairie, away!"[17]

Less akin to showmanship, yet appealing to an equally large and enthusiastic public, were the works of narrative painters of the West who thrived at mid-century. The paintings of Arthur F. Tait, William Ranney and Charles Deas received broad popular dissemination as prints by Currier & Ives and the Western Art-Union. Variations on one theme alone, "the trapper's last shot," were explored by Stanley, Tait, Deas, Ranney and Louis Maurer, among others. Versions of most of these received distribution in print form. The popularity of such episodic accounts was evidence of a continuing—in fact, growing—demand for the frontier adventure and wilderness drama of the Wild West.

Eventually, nature herself was introduced. With the post-Civil War press westward, artists toting paint boxes and white umbrellas paraded to the Rockies to glory in their silhouette. "In nature, as in human life, nothing is impossible,"[18] wrote Albert Richardson in 1869. The West's premier landscape artist, Albert Bierstadt, proved that the painter, given enough canvas, coul expand on even that lofty concept. Some observers suggested his paintings were greater than all outdoors. Others, like the art critic James Jackson Jarves, commented that the public might confuse such masterworks as *The Rocky Mountains* with a panorama, wondering as they pondered the huge canvas just when *"the thing was going to move?"*[19] Despite his being roundly criticized for these monumental *tours de force,* Bierstadt's place as the most popul American artist of the nineteenth century was incontestable.

Such a work as the *Storm in the Rocky Mountains* was "to be

Left:
Albert Bierstadt
Yellowstone Falls n.d.
Oil on canvas
112.4 x 77.5 cm. (44¼ x 30½ in.)
*Collection: Buffalo Bill Historical Center,
Cody, Wyoming*

Center:
An Eadweard Muybridge photograph of
Bierstadt at Mariposa, California, 1878
*Courtesy California Historical Society,
San Francisco*

Bottom:
An engraving of *The Last Lull in the Fight*
by Remington, from *Harper's Weekly,*
March 30, 1889

considered an epic of landscape art."[20] So strong was the impact of the "grand" and the sublime in such paintings that viewers approached them as high drama. And though this style was in no way exclusive in its application to the Rockies, its most monumental form came from the Far West.

Most of the "grand" style landscapes were painted in total focus so that details of foreground and distance could be identified with equal clarity. This practice allowed the paintings to be viewed with opera glasses, thus effecting a sense of on-the-spot observation and allying the experience very closely with that of theater.[21] Accordingly, the major works of Bierstadt were as much popular entertainment as works of art. The "wild" in Bierstadt's Wild West expositions was the wilderness—its grandeur and its sublimity.

That such an approach did not endure is explained as much by the dynamics of the frontier as by the changes in artistic and popular taste. By the time Bierstadt had passed from fashion in the late 1880s, the West had been transformed by successive waves of history and humanity; the "wild" had gradually been tamed and the frontier confronted its demise. What the public demanded at this juncture was a recap of that which had passed so quickly. The ubiquitous illustrated journals of the day filled the void and in the interpretation of the West, the illustrators took command.

Frederic Remington, who operated in the provinces of both illustration and fine art, brought the American and European public those Western images they longed to remember. In 1889, the most important year in Remington's career, he had five paintings accepted for the Paris Universal Exposition. An oil titled *A Lull in the Fight* won for him a silver medal.

That tastes were changing is seen in the fact that Bierstadt's monumental painting, *The Last of the Buffalo*, was rejected by the same committee that accepted the five Remington works. George C. Brown, a member of the selection committee, expressed the tenor of the current artistic disposition. ''I believe . . . that American artists . . . should paint the things of interest they see around them, and pay no attention to those who call them commonplace . . .''[22] For Remington this was natural; for Bierstadt, anathema.

So Remington and his Realist colleagues took the stage, and since by this time the frontier had essentially closed, they explored subjects that covered its whole history. Once this chapter of the Western saga had ended, the public demanded more and more—and it was up to Remington to supply. He proved up to the task. ''It is a fact that admits of no question,'' wrote critic William Coffin in 1892, ''that Eastern people have formed their conceptions of what the Far-Western life is like, more from what they have seen in Mr. Remington's pictures than from any other source.''[23]

Unlike Catlin or Stanley or even Bierstadt, Remington never turned to theater in his art and he did not have to. There were two good reasons. First, his illustrations in *Harper's Weekly*, *Scribner's*, *Century* and other magazines touched such a vast audience that the artist could remain comparatively isolated and still

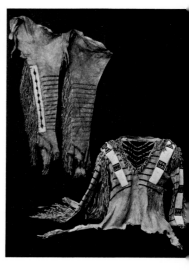

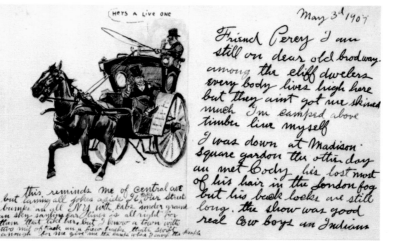

Left:
Albert Bierstadt
Sketch for **The Last of the Buffalo**
circa 1889
Oil on board
36.5 x 48.2 cm. (14⅜ x 19 in.)
Collection: Buffalo Bill Historical Center, Cody, Wyoming

Below:
A man's shirt and leggings, collected by Remington from the Blackfeet, *circa* 1850
Collection: Buffalo Bill Historical Center, Cody, Wyoming

Left:
Charles Marion Russell
He's a Live One 1907
Pen and ink, watercolor
15.9 x 24.5 cm. (6¼ x 9⅝ in.)
Collection: Buffalo Bill Historical Center, Cody, Wyoming

Below:
The Wild West show at Ambrose Park, South Brooklyn, *circa* 1894
Courtesy Long Island Historical Society, New York

Right:
Rosa Bonheur
Col. W. F. Cody 1889
Oil on canvas
47.0 x 38.7 cm. (18½ x 15¼ in.)
*Collection: Buffalo Bill Historical Center,
Cody, Wyoming*

Below:
Charles Schreyvogel
The Summit Springs Rescue—1869
1908
Oil on canvas
121.9 x 167.6 cm. (48 x 66 in.)
*Collection: Buffalo Bill Historical Center,
Cody, Wyoming*

succeed. Secondly, Buffalo Bill and later showmen of the Western scene adopted the theater element as their own province, thus freeing Remington to pursue a more refined if less dramatic medium.

In the autumn of 1894 Remington and a friend, Julian Ralph, attended the Wild West show in Brooklyn. Thirty fenced acres corralled "Buffalo Bill's camp"[24] of Rough riders. Remington had long shared Cody's affinity for the multiform horsemen of the world, but he and Ralph had come primarily to see the Indians. They found to their satisfaction that, though "mainly Sioux," the Indians had "the conspicuous merit that belongs to all parts of this show—that of being genuine."[25] Such an observation was important to both showman and artist, for in their separate domains they each strove to achieve their own relative authenticity.

Remington was a friend of Cody's and painted a number of pictures of him. Other artists also enjoyed Cody's patronage. Charles Schreyvogel was commissioned to paint *The Summit Springs Rescue.* The artist was paid in mining stock and one painted Sioux tipi. The stock was never redeemed as the mine failed. The tipi, however, remained an integral part of Schreyvogel's studio effects. Rosa Bonheur cherished Cody's company and savored the image of Buffalo Bill and his entourage. Her portraits of the showman and the various members of the group reveal a sense of unity between the French artist and the Wild West characters. In her studio the mounted head of Buffalo Bill's horse Tucker hung proudly over the hearth, and the walls were decorated with Indian paraphernalia procured from Native American members of the troupe. Charles Russell, N.C. Wyeth and many other turn-of-the-century artists also portrayed elements of Cody's

adventurous life. Detroit painter Irving R. Bacon was one who did numerous commissioned works for Cody. His allegorical *Conquest of the Prairie* evokes the passing of America's frontier with Buffalo Bill figuring prominently in that destiny. As Cody symbolized the Western saga, artists could readily find in him and his Wild West shows subjects for their canvases.

Cody functioned as both patron and inspiration for a world of artists. His imagery, drawn from myth and history and the reenactment of both, became universal. If the aphorism "history exists as a force because it is created here and now" has credence, then Buffalo Bill and the

artists associated with him have served history well. They provided an avenue through which society could respond to itself and its recent past. They opened the West to the world of their day and preserved its elemental spirit for the generations to follow.

Top:
Irving R. Bacon
Conquest of the Prairie 1908
Oil on canvas
120.0 x 301.0 cm. (47¼ x 118½ in.)
Collection: Buffalo Bill Historical Center, Cody, Wyoming

Above:
Thomas Moran
The Grand Canyon of the Yellowstone 1875
Chromolithograph
Image size: 27.3 x 38.1 cm.
(10¾ x 15 in.)
Collection: Buffalo Bill Historical Center, Cody, Wyoming

1-4.   Frederic Remington, "Buffalo Bill in London," *Harper's Weekly,* September 3, 1892, p. 847.

5.   Charles C. Sellers, *The Artist of the Revolution: The Early Life of Charles Willson Peale* (Hebron, CT, 1939), p. 270.

6.   See Wolfgang Born, *American Landscape Painting* (Westport, CT, 1948), p. 75.

7.   See Lee Parry, "Landscape Theater in America," *Art in America,* November-December, 1971, pp. 52-55. The original studies for Trumbull's Niagara Falls are in the collection of the New York Historical Society, New York, NY.

8.   George Catlin, *Catalogue of Catlin's Indian Gallery of Portraits, Landscapes, Manners and Customs, Costumes, &c. &c . . .* (New York, 1837), p. 40.

9.   George Catlin, *Letters and Notes on the North American Indians,* ed. Michael M. Mooney (New York, 1975), p. 61.

10.   See George Catlin, *Adventures of the Ojibeway and Ioway Indians in England, France, and Belgium . . .*, 2 vols. (London, 1852).

11.   Marvin C. Ross, *The West of Alfred Jacob Miller* (Norman, OK, 1968), facing p. 110.

12.   Mathew C. Field, *Prairie and Mountain Sketches* (Norman, OK, 1957), p. 150.

13.   "Indians," *New York Tribune,* November 28, 1850, p. 6.

14.   "Stanley's Indian Gallery," *New York Tribune,* January 23, 1851, p. 5.

15.   "Indian Gallery of Paintings," *National Intelligencer,* February 23, 1852, p. 4.

16.   "Western Wilds," *Washington Daily Evening Star,* December 11, 1854, p. 3.

17.   John Mix Stanley, *Scenes and Incidents of Stanley's Western Wilds* (Washington, DC, 1854), p. 1.

18.   Albert D. Richardson, *Beyond the Mississippi* (Hartford, CT, 1869), p. 497.

19.   James Jackson Jarves, *The Art Idea,* ed. Benjamin Rowland, Jr. (Cambridge, MA, 1960), p. 205.

20.   "Fine Arts," *The Illustrated London News,* June 15, 1867, p. 599.

21.   See E.A. Carmean, Jr., *Nature and Focus* (Houston, 1972), p. 10.

22.   J.G. Brown, "American Subjects for American Artists," *New York Herald,* March 31, 1889.

23.   William A. Coffin, "American Illustration of To-day," *Scribner's Magazine,* March, 1892, p. 348.

24-25.   Julian Ralph, "Behind the 'Wild West' Scenes," *Harper's Weekly,* September 1, 1894, p. 775.

Buffalo Bill and the Wild West

The Wild West"

Richard Slotkin

*Wesleyan University
Middletown, Connecticut*

Buffalo Bill's Wild West was one of the most remarkable entertainments ever staged. The impressive size of the undertaking, the enormity of the audiences, the complex logistics of moving hundreds of animals and performers on trains or transoceanic liners—all suggest a level of business operation far beyond the relatively simple life of a frontier scout. Cody's Wild West show was a reflection of popular taste from 1883 to 1913. The pressure to draw large crowds required the extensive use of commercial promotional systems and popular media, and, as in the world of entertainment today, the development of subject matter and story lines that would satisfy the curiosity and desires of the mass audience. Richard Slotkin focuses on Cody's extravaganza as a many-layered vehicle for conveying history, romantic fantasies and political ideologies. [DHK]

Poster
Westward, The Course of Empire 1898
Printer: Enquirer Job Printing Co.,
Cincinnati, Ohio
28-sheet: 287.0 x 735.0 cm.
(112 x 287 in.)
*Collection: Circus World Museum of
Baraboo, Wisconsin.
From 100 Posters of Buffalo Bill's Wild
West by Jack Rennert, Copyright 1976
Darien House, Inc.*

Our sense of history is a mixture of the factual and the mythological. When we recall the story of the past we often emphasize or focus on events, figures and themes that have been traditionally invested with a special symbolic significance. These foci of heightened symbolism I would call *myths.*

Among our national myths the longest-lived and most persistent has been the "Myth of the Frontier," which represents the story of expansion westward into the wilderness as the key to all that is meaningful in American history. When Frederick Jackson Turner codified this myth as a coherent and respectable theory of history in 1893, it had already been part of the intellectual and literary landscape for nearly two centuries. According to the myth, the process of westward expansion was the stimulus that drove the American economy on a persistent upward course of development. The project of expansion provoked the disagreements that led to Civil War; but it also made for the growth of nationalist sentiment. By offering free land to farmers it made political democracy possible and economic equity feasible. By replacing Indians with "civilized" settlers, it expanded the borders of civilization against a supposed "savagery." When the frontier finally "closed" at the end of the nineteenth century, America no longer had a magic safety valve for avoiding industrial and urban social conflicts—the moment is imagined in the myth as a kind of "expulsion from Eden," followed by sweat, poverty and strife.

All of these premises are now seen as factually and morally questionable; but they constituted a public system of belief for much of our history, and that they persist in some form today, seems beyond dispute.[1]

The heroes of the frontier myth were historical characters whose real accomplishments formed the core around which folk legends and the more subtle fictions of historians and romance-writers grew. Preeminent among them were the wilderness hunters and Indian fighters, the often solitary plebeian adventurers who blazed the trails into the world of the Indian, the grizzly and the buffalo. There are innumerable fictional versions of this figure—beginning with Cooper's famous Leatherstocking—and numerous historical hunter-warriors whose deeds earned them a measure of fame. But four names dominate the field and define the type: Daniel Boone, Davy Crockett, Kit Carson and "Buffalo Bill" Cody. They share a common status as symbolic forerunners of the advancing bourgeois democracy of the United States. Through this myth of the hunter, Americans have symbolically reconciled their contradictory responses to their own social form, their love-hate response to industrial civilization and its discontents. The hunter speaks for the values and pleasures of a "natural" and "unfettered" precapitalist Eden. Yet he facilitates the spread of "progress" and "civilization," and himself embodies the agressive go-getter spirit, the willful and dominant temperment, the pragmatic turn of mind, and the belief in racial superiority that characterized ninteenth-century bourgeois culture.

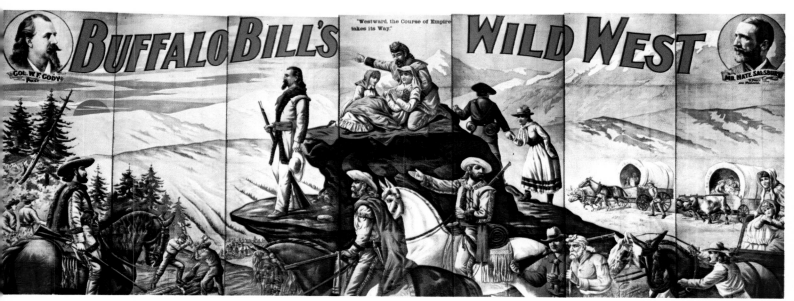

Above:
C. H. Stephens
Hunting Buffalo 1911
Oil on canvas
45.7 x 55.9 cm. (18 x 22 in.)
Collection: Buffalo Bill Historical Center, Cody, Wyoming

Right and below:
Last of the Great Scouts by Helen Cody Wetmore—Cody's sister—published in 1899, and Buffalo Bill dime novels by Col. Prentiss Ingraham
Collection: Buffalo Bill Historical Center, Cody, Wyoming

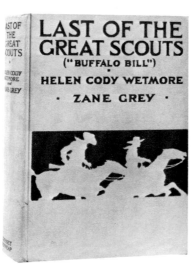

Within this general structure, the four heroes represent four different periods of frontier expansion: Boone the earliest phase of agrarian development west of the Appalachians; Crockett the Jacksonian phase, in which class and sectional conflicts surfaced in the backwash of a temporarily "closed" frontier; Carson the phase of renewed expansion that followed the Mexican War and the Gold Rush of '49. Buffalo Bill is typically presented as the "last" of the type—the "Last of the Great Scouts," the "Last of the Plainsmen"—for his period saw the coming of the railroad to the Plains, the binding of Wild West to civilized East, the last of the Indian wars, the last of the Western gold and land "rushes." However, more than terminal position sets Buffalo Bill apart from the rest of this pantheon.

Although his legend shares many important elements with those of the other hunter heroes, it is unique in that its development occurred in the period of American industrialization and overseas imperialism. This affected both the content of the myth, and the cultural context in which it existed; it also affected the forms through which the myth was transmitted, by providing new and unique resources for making and marketing the legend. Cody was unique in his ability to exploit and manage this new popular culture marketplace. Boone, Crockett and Carson tried in differing degrees to cash in on their fame by the production of autobiographical narratives or ghostwritten biographies, which appeared as pamphlets and books during their lifetimes. But most of the profit in their names was reaped by hack writers and dime novelists. Cody had a more complex and wide-ranging literary market at his disposal, and he proved an astute entrepreneur in controlling what became a minor industry turning out

Buffalo Bill dime novels, biographies, annuals, serials and anthologies. And none of his predecessors had either the inspiration, the capital resources, the logistical capability or the available audience to mount anything like the Wild West show.

Cody's mastery of the media involved more than business talent and impresario's flair. Cody (and the people closest to him) also had a unique perspective on the phenomenon of "living legendry" in general, and of "frontier hero" status in particular. He understood, and played upon, the deep vein of nostalgia for a precapitalist "paradise" that had always been at the heart of the frontier myth. He understood also that the myth of the frontier was not exclusively a Western myth, but rather a national myth, and one that was especially dear to the ideologists and literary entrepreneurs of the metropolitan East, who used it as the basis of romantic fiction and of no less romantic political ideologies. Cody's mythmaking succeeded by linking the mythologized history of the "vanishing" frontier to the major tendencies of contemporary economic and political life—the triumph of industrialism over agrarianism, and the beginning of American imperialism overseas.

□   □

Cody made his legend at first by exploiting parallels between his career and those of the earlier hunter heroes. But as the West and the nation changed, he modified the legends, altered his roles and costume, and even acted on the historical stage in such a way as to suggest that Buffalo Bill was a symbolic conduit through which the heroism of the frontier past could be transmitted to modern America. The dime novels and "biographies" of Buffalo Bill emphasized the Boone-Carson-Crockett aspects of

SHOOTING GLASS BALLS

HUNTING BUFFALO

Above:
Poster
From Prairie to Palace *circa* 1887
Printer: Russell-Morgan Printing Co.,
Cincinnati, Ohio
71 x 102 cm. (28 x 40 in.)
*Collection: Buffalo Bill Historical Center,
Cody, Wyoming*

Above, right:
Buffalo Bill in his 7th Cavalry uniform,
circa 1880
*Courtesy Buffalo Bill Historical Center,
Cody, Wyoming*

Below:
Buffalo Bill's Vengeance, a pulp novel by
Col. Prentiss Ingraham
*Collection: Buffalo Bill Historical Center,
Cody, Wyoming*

Below right:
Wild Bill Hickok, New York, *circa* 1875
*Courtesy Buffalo Bill Historical Center,
Cody, Wyoming*

Cody's boyhood and career as a scout. But they did not conceal or slight the fact that Cody's great deeds were performed as an employee in the service of an industrial corporation—the Kansas Pacific Railroad—rather than as an independent, yeoman farmer-hunter or free mountain man. Cody's success as a capitalist in the East was as much celebrated by dime biographer Prentiss Ingraham as his riding a wild buffalo; and later dime novels showed Cody not merely as a forerunner of Railroad America, but as successfully integrated into the new order. He began his dime-novel career fighting Indians to avenge Custer, and ended as a kind of gentleman detective in books like *Buffalo Bill and the Nihilists* (1910), in which he protects a visiting Russian Grand Duke from assassination. Far from resisting the transition from "frontier" to "modern" America, Cody assimilated it into the body of his personal myth.[2]

Such an assimilation was not easily made credible. Part of the deep emotional appeal of the frontier hero is the belief that he is an anachronism, a figure from a lost national childhood. The first great fictional embodiment of the figure—Cooper's Leatherstocking—is always spoken of as the last of a vanishing breed, and when Owen Wister in his novel *The Virginian* (1902), sought to envision such a hero making the transition to modernity, he acknowledged that the ambition put a strain on the material—the virtues and skills of dime-novel hunters and cowboys are not readily transformed into those of entrepreneurial capitalists.[3]

Cody made his own transition credible by ingeniously interweaving mythic symbolism with authenticating touches of historicity. The achievement was based on an understanding of the processes that first made him a celebrity. Until 1869

Cody had been a minor actor on the stage of Western history, a boy- and man-of-all-work who had been teamster, drover, soldier, Pony Express rider, deputy, meat hunter and army scout. The upsurge of Eastern interest in the Plains that followed the commencement of work on the transcontinental railroad brought numerous journalists, gentlemen-hunters, and dime novelists like Ned Buntline to the scene of the action. There was money to be made guiding such folk on hunting trips, and fame to be garnered and exploited when these trips were written up back East. Wild Bill Hickok and Cody both achieved early fame in this way—Hickok in a magazine article written for *Harper's Monthly* by G.W. Nichols, Cody in a Buntline dime novel published in 1869 and a stage melodrama that premiered in 1872. Dime-novel celebrity made Cody a figure to be sought out by visiting Easterners, increasing journalistic interest in his ongoing career as scout and guide.

EN ROUTE

AGAIN WE GREET YOU

And this time with the GREATEST DRAMATIC ATTRACTION ever presented to a Theatre Going Public. Most Extraordinary Success has attended

THE ILLUSTRIOUS GOVERNMENT SCOUT,

BUFFALO BILL

SIOUX CHIEFS!

SIOUX CHIEFS!

(HON. W. F. CODY,) AND HIS

COMBINATION

During their recent visits to PHILADELPHIA, BALTIMORE, WASHINGTON and NEW YORK, where, even the largest Opera Houses have been incapable of accommodating the masses, and in which latter city a re engagement was made at the New and Capacious EAGLE THEATRE, which was packed nightly with the elite,

To witness the Most Refined and Meritorious SENSATIONAL DRAMA ever written, entitled

MAY CODY

OR, LOST AND WON.

Written expressly for Hon. W F. CODY, (Buffalo Bill) by MAJ. A. S. BURT, U. S. A.

SYNOPSIS OF SCENERY AND INCIDENTS:

ACT FIRST. Scene 1st.—Drawing-room in Mrs Stoughton's Residence, 5th Avenue. The anonymous letter. The Secretary dismissed. Searching for the Lost Sister. The Faithful Footman. The Rescue. Tableau.

ACT SECOND. Scene 1st.—Echo Canyon. Dead Man's Cave. Utah Territory. Brigham Young and John D. Lee. The Prophet's Danites. Kill! Kill! Kill! Remember Negroes! Dennis and his Donkey. The Unwelcome Visitor. Bill's Encounter with a Grizzly. Arrival of the Camp Train. THE SIOUX CHIEFS. The Austin Brothers. The Experts Entertain the Party with some Skillful Shooting. John D. Lee, alias California Joe. Treachery. The Atrocious Mountain Meadows Massacre. Scene 2d.—Darby and the Danite. Abduction "Is there a Chance to Save Her." Scene 3d.—The Silent Oath. Tableau.

ACT THIRD. Scene 1st.—May Cody and Brigham Young. Timely Arrival of White Wolf. Lee's Proposal. "Yield!" "Never!" Scene 2d.—The Endowment Chamber of the Lion House. The Initiation of the New Candidate. Nipped in the Bud. Tableau. Scene 3d.—The Pursuit. The Duel. TABLEAU.

ACT FOURTH. Scene 1st.—Fort Bridger. The Garrison. General Harney's Quarters. Arrival of Bill. An Agreeable Surprise. "What the Degradation Has on Your Head!" Finding the Report. "Who can I Trust." A Drumhead Court Martial. Scene 2d.—The Fatiguing Journey. Darby Discovers Fort Bridger. "We are Saved!" Scene 3d.—In the Guard House. Mrs. Stoughton's Interview. The Story of the Past. "Hold! Spare the Lady!" The Intercession. "Good Bye, All!" "Ready!—Aim.!" "This is my Trick, Bill Cody!" "Fire." Lee Unmasked. His Escape. Two Bears Farewell. The Interception. "Good Bye, All!" "Ready!—Aim.!" "This is my Trick, Bill Cody!" "Fire." Lee Unmasked. His Escape. Two Bears and Cha-Sha-Sha-o-pogeo on his Trail. Dennis Proven an Able. "Forget and Forgive; for Life has Lost and I have Won." Tableau.

Incidental to the Play, will be the Introduction of the RED MEN OF THE FAR WEST,

TWO BEARS, And the Indian Scout and Interpreter. CHA-SHA-SHA-O-POGEO

— ON THEIR —

TRAINED BRONCHO PONIES, and the Mexican Trick Bouro, JACK CASS

SEE OPINIONS OF PRESS.

The Drama, MAY CODY; or, LOST AND WON, though of a highly exampled character is carefully blended with comedy of the highest order, painted by delicacy and correct Diningse, unexampled by beautiful scenery and incidents and impressions; and imaginative interpolation—a succession of features to perfect as to fill almost the counterpart of the events it describes.—*N Y Herald.*

The Drama, May Cody, introducing Buffalo Bill, the Sioux Chief and other attractions that have been presented nightly for the past few weeks at Ford's Grand Opera House, is certainly the great entertainment of the season.—*Baltimore Sun.*

Quite an ovation was tendered to Hon. W. F. Cody (Buffalo Bill), at Ford's Opera-House last evening. The house was densely packed, and all the private boxes were occupied by the visiting Indian Delegates, accompanied by Gen. Crook, Gen. Henry, and other distinguished officials.—*Washington Republican.*

☞ The Company is composed of ARTISTS OF WELL-KNOWN ABILITY, carefully Selected Including the Popular Comedian, **THOS. Z. GRAHAM,** Who will be pleasantly remembered last season as DENNIS O'GAFF

JOSEPH WINTER,	J. P. RAYMOND,	HARRY MELMER,
JOHN HARVEY,	J. S. BROWNING,	W. S. MacEVOY,
GEO. C. CHARLES,	JOS. V. ARLINGTON,	GEO. H. STEVENS,
J. Y. NELSON,	Miss ADA FORRESTER,	Mrs. G. C. CHARLES,
Miss M. S. JONES,		Miss ANNA WALL.

Also, the World-Renowned

AUSTIN BROTHERS

The CRACK RIFLE TEAM of the world, who have been engaged to more faithfully portray the Realistic Incidents.

In Panoramic Order will be given ENTIRE NEW SCENERY and APPOINTMENTS, with THRILLING TABLEAUX.

MOUNTAIN MEADOWS MASSACRE.

BRIGHAM YOUNG'S TEMPLE

Or, as familiarly known at Salt Lake, "THE LION HOUSE."

The Danites! The Danites!   The Endowment Chamber.
General Harney's Quarters.   The Garrison at Fort Bridger.

A DRUMHEAD COURT-MARTIAL.

The Play is Beautifully Mounted with New Scenery, Wardrobe, Natural Costumes, Mechanical Properties, etc. FOR PARTICULARS, POPULAR PRICES, &c. SEE DAILY PAPERS.

HON. W. F. CODY,	Proprietor and Manager	J. P. RAYMOND,	Leader of Orchestra
CHAS. E. BLANCHETT,	Business Manager	JOSH K. OGDEN,	General Equipment Agent
J. S. WINTER,	Stage Manager	CHAS. J. THORNE,	Assistant Agent

NOROMBEGA HALL, - - Bangor.

FRIDAY & SATURDAY, November 9th and 10th, '77.

acing page, left:
n 1877 "Buffalo Bill Combination"
oster
ollection: Buffalo Bill Historical Center,
ody, Wyoming

acing page, top right:
eorge Armstrong Custer, Grand Duke
lexis of Russia and Cody during the
rince's 1872 visit to the West
ourtesy Buffalo Bill Historical Center,
ody, Wyoming

acing page, bottom right:
led Buntline, Buffalo Bill, Giuseppina
1orlacchi and Texas Jack Omohundro
s they appeared in the 1872 melodrama
he Scouts of the Prairie; or Red Deviltry
s It Is
ourtesy Buffalo Bill Historical Center,
ody, Wyoming

elow:
uffalo Bill, circa 1877, in a black velvet
1exican suit
ourtesy Buffalo Bill Historical Center,
ody, Wyoming

As a result, his service as guide for the famous Buffalo Hunt of the Grand Duke Alexis in 1872 became an event of national celebrity. James Gordon Bennett, Jr., publisher of the popular and sensational New York *Herald,* first exploited Cody journalistically and then employed him as a scout for his own hunting party. He followed this by inviting Cody to come to New York, hoping for a futher social and journalistic bonanza; and Cody, at the urging of his army superiors and friends, seized the opportunity to cash in on his celebrity. His visit to the East was a success for Bennett; Cody himself moved to take control of the commodity of his fame by seeking out Ned Buntline and forming a kind of partnership for the production of Buffalo Bill dime novels and stage melodramas.

Between 1872 and 1876 Cody alternated between his career as scout and guide on the Plains, and his business as star of a series of stage melodramas in the East. His theatrical enterprises generally prospered, and he formed his own "Buffalo Bill Combination" with Wild Bill Hickok and Texas Jack Omohundro in 1873. While the melodramas themselves were trivial, and the acting not of the highest quality, Cody had discovered that public interest could be aroused by the association of familiar dime-novel or melodrama figures with authentic representatives of the frontier.

He had thus established the perfect position from which to exploit the golden opportunity offered by the events of 1876. In that year General Custer—with whom Cody had been briefly associated—was wiped out by the Sioux and Cheyennes in the famous Last Stand at the Little Big Horn. Cody was scheduled to return to the Plains that summer as Chief of Scouts for Colonel Merritt's 5th Cavalry; he used the news of the Last Stand as the occasion for announcing his farewell to the stage, and declaring an intention to get "the first scalp for Custer." He then reported to Merritt, and in the skirmish at War Bonnet Creek later that summer killed and scalped a Cheyenne named Yellow Hand. Cody had attired himself in anticipation of the battle in the ornate Mexican costume he affected on stage; when he returned to the East, he could appear in his proper stage costume and declare honestly that he was wearing the very clothes he had worn when he "avenged Custer."[4] The picture of Cody waving aloft the "first scalp" adorned Buffalo Bill dime novels and Wild West programs for years afterwards, and the grisly souvenir itself was displayed outside the theater, outraging the Friends-of-the-Indian group in Boston, titillating sensation seekers, and augmenting the mystique of Buffalo Bill as an authentic Indian fighter of the Plains.

Above:
Robert Lindneux
First Scalp for Custer 1928
Oil on canvas
182.9 x 426.8 cm. (72 x 168 in.)
*Collection: Buffalo Bill Historical Center,
Cody, Wyoming*

Right:
Buffalo Bill's display of the Cheyenne leader Yellow Hand's scalp, war bonnet, shield, gun, belt and scabbard
*Courtesy Buffalo Bill Historical Center,
Cody, Wyoming*

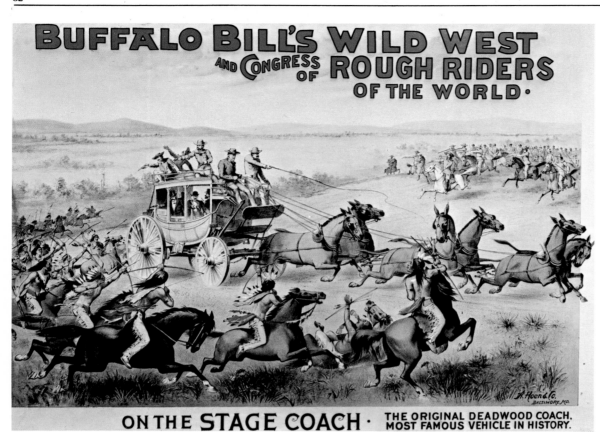

Left, top:
Poster
On the Stage Coach *circa* 1887
Printer: A. Hoen & Co., Baltimore, Maryland
71 x 98 cm. (28 x 38½ in.)
Collection: Buffalo Bill Historical Center, Cody, Wyoming

Left, center:
Buffalo Bill and General Nelson A. Miles view an Indian camp near Pine Ridge, South Dakota, January 16, 1891. At right are Captain Frank D. Baldwin and Captain Marion P. Maus.
Courtesy National Archives, Washington D.C.

Left, bottom:
Sitting Bull, the famous Sioux spiritual leader, and Cody, 1885
Courtesy The Denver Public Library, Western History Department, Colorado

Below:
Cover of a 1907 Wild West program
Collection: Buffalo Bill Historical Center, Cody, Wyoming

ere the Buffalo Bill signature ppears clearly, in a characteristic onfusion of the theatrical and the al. The real adventure in the West framed by theater—the speech efore the footlights, the costume, e exploitation after the fact. Yet the eed itself is, unquestionably, real''—blood is shed, a battle is on, Cody's commander mentions m in dispatches, the newspapers raise him. Cody validates his ctional performances by reference real deeds, and makes those eeds comprehensible to an Eastern udience by linking them with the nly "West" with which they are amiliar: the mythic West of melodrama and dime novels.

He was to repeat the pattern in 890, when he interrupted a tour vith the Wild West to attempt mediation with Sitting Bull on the ve of the Ghost Dance outbreak. Although his diplomacy was hwarted, the Wild West show of 893 invoked the Ghost Dance dventure at every opportunity.[5]

□   □

The effect of Cody's assimilation of uistory to melodrama is to reduce (or nflate) historical moments to archetypal status. They cease to epresent contingent events, and become embodiments of timeless and typical struggles between forces and figures that are emblematic of progress and right against savagery and evil. In his conception of the Wild West show, Cody found the perfect vehicle for achieving this effect, and the successive versions of he Wild West suggest that he was or became fully conscious of the show's possibilities as a mythmaking medium.

The Wild West began in 1883 as a rodeo-like display of "Cowboy Fun," including feats of marksmanship, riding and roping, nterspersed with races and framed

by parades. To this were added elements that would appeal to the larger public's enthusiam for the mythical and historical West of dime novels and sensational journalism. In the first years of the show, a number of "spectacles" were developed which offered "authentic" reenactments of scenes from Western life and history, including war dances by Indians, the Pony Express, an attack on a settlers' cabin, another attack by Indians on Deadwood stagecoach, and a "Grand [Buffalo] Hunt on the Plains" reminiscent of the Grand Duke's expedition of 1872. The iconography and subject matter of these scenes were derived from Buffalo Bill legendry—that is , from historical events as filtered through the distorting lens of Buffalo Bill dime novels and journalistic "puffs." A good deal of attention was given to establishing an impression of authenticity in the representation of the frontier. This was accomplished by the presence of historical celebrities like Major North of the Pawnee Battalion, Sheriff Con Groner, Sitting Bull (in 1885—86), Rain-in-the-Face—and of course Buffalo Bill himself. But the illusion of authenticity was reinforced as well by the conformity between Wild West scenes and the audience expectations created by the prevalence of the very inauthentic dime-novel version of the West.[6]

The season of 1886 marks a watershed in the development of the Wild West formula. In that year the show was offered as "America's National Entertainment," and an exemplification of the entire course of American history. An elaborate program, densely packed with text and lavishly illustrated, was distributed as advertising for the show and as a guide to the action for the audience. These programs went beyond the merely descriptive to provide a historical and ideological

Cover of an 1886 Wild West program.
Collection: The Denver Public Library, Western History Department, Colorado

King Leopold II of Belgium (far right) visits Cody at his headquarters tent during the Wild West's 1887 European tour.
Courtesy The Denver Public Library, Western History Department, Colorado

rationale for the show. They argued seriously for its value as an educational enterprise and as a patriotic pageant. When the show made its first European tour in 1887, the prospect of the confrontation between New World and Old provoked even more strenuous efforts to articulate this rationale, as demonstrated by John M. Burke's "Salutatory" preface—a permanent feature of the programs.

It is the aim of the management of Buffalo Bill's Wild West to do more than present an exacting and realistic entertainment for the public amusement. Their object is to PICTURE TO THE EYE, by the aid of historical characters and living animals, a series of animated scenes and episodes, which had their existence in fact, of the wonderful pioneer and frontier life of the Wild West of America.

Beginning with the Primeval Forest, peopled by the Indian and Wild Beasts only, the story of the gradual civilization of a vast continent is depicted. The hardships, daring, and frontier skill of the participants being a guarantee of the faithful reproduction of scenes and incidents in which they had actual experience.

The central figure in these pictures is that of THE HON. W.F. CODY (Buffalo Bill), to whose sagacity, skill, energy, and courage . . . the settlers of the West owe so much for the reclamation of the prairie from the savage Indian and wild animals, who so long opposed the march of civilization.

Attention to the Orator will materially assist the spectator in his grasp of the leading episodes.[7]

The show was organized around "spectacles" which purported to reenact scenes from different "Epochs" of American history. The first "Epoch" displayed the show's

Indian dancers, but framed their performance as typifying life in "the Primeval Forest" before the coming of the white man. Later segments displayed the landing of the Pilgrims or John Smith and Pocahontas. Still later "Epochs" moved directly from Plymouth Rock to the Plains, showing life on a cattle ranch. The "Buffalo Hunt" and the attacks on the settlers' cabin and the Deadwood stagecoach were repeated, but were framed as historical events typical of the later "Epochs" of American history. "Cowboy Fun" was set between the "Epochs," and also provided the main action for sequences like that of the "Cattle Ranch." There were also spectacular "special effects" scenes, including a prairie fire, a sunset and a cyclone.[8]

The program's insistence on the historicity of its "Epochs" and the "educational value" of the performance must be taken seriously. Although it is clear that the primary attraction of the show as entertainment lay in the "circus" and "spectacular" features, even the "special effects" are justified as adding "realism" to the performance. But this kind of realism is akin to the use of celebrity performers in that it uses "real" elements to authenticate an illusion. The historical program has little to do with real historical stages or moments. The "history" reenacted here is mythic; it moves directly from the Fenimore Cooper myth of the "Forest Primeval" to the Buffalo Bill dime-novel myth of the Plains, with no intervening stages. American history is simply subsumed in the story of the frontier—and the story of the frontier is subsumed in mythology of popular fiction. The reenactments do not re-create

events; they reduce complexes of historical happenings to "typical scenes," and ritually reenact these "types."

It is the most extraordinary tribute to Cody's skill that his educational pretensions were taken seriously, and his manipulation of illusions received as authentic. According to Brick Pomeroy, a journalist quoted in the program, the show ought to have been titled "Wild West Reality," because it had "more of real life, of genuine interest, of positive education" than "all of this imaginary Romeo and Juliet business." Pomeroy wished "there were more progressive educators like William Cody in this world." Pomeroy's blurb was as much a part of the "credentials" Cody offered in his program as were the testimonials of the Generals under whom he had served as a scout.[9]

But the Wild West show was not reality. It created a mythic space, in which reality and legend, past and present could coexist. It made history into ritual, by acting out the myths that had been made of history. Its power was such that when, in 1887, it produced a reenactment of an indubitably historical event—Custer's Last Stand—it assimilated the historical event to the myth with virtuoso facility. And this appetite for assimilating history was extended, over the years, even to current events.

☐   ☐

The Wild West show returned from a second European tour to become a major attraction operating in tandem with the Columbian Exposition of 1893. It was during this year that the

Wild West made over a million dollars in profit. The Exposition was designed to display the industrial and political accomplishments of America in the four centuries since its discovery, and its emphasis was clearly on the present and future glory of the states. Its "White City" of pavilions and halls presented the future in utopian terms.

Below:
Buffalo Bill in his Wild West show costume, *circa* 1893
Courtesy Buffalo Bill Historical Center, Cody, Wyoming

Left:
Royal jewelry: A gold pocket watch with crown design in diamonds given to Cody by King Victor Emmanuel of Italy in 1899; a set of diamond studded gold stickpin and rings given by Grand Duke Alexis of Russia in 1872; a gold brooch with diamonds and "R" on the front given by Queen Victoria in 1892; and a gold watch engraved with buffalo and illustration of Cody on the sides, together with a gold fob with amethyst, given by King Edward VII in 1890
Collection: Buffalo Bill Historical Center, Cody, Wyoming

Buffalo Bill's WILD WEST

....AND....

CONGRESS OF ROUGH RIDERS OF THE WORLD

Return to America After Six Years

Triumphant Tour of Europe

Visited and Indorsed by the Potentates and People of All Countries.

Unequaled in the History of Amusements

Positively the Largest and Most Complete Outdoor Exhibition in the World

VIVID AND REALISTIC SCENES

FROM THE

PIONEER HISTORY OF AMERICA.

100 Indians ∫ Sioux, Comanche, Pawnee and Blackfeet.
75 Cowboys.
50 Mexican Vanqueros.
25 South American Gauchos.
25 Rio Grande Cabaliero.
25 Mexican Rurale, and Others.

MOUNTED BATTALIONS REPRESENTING THE

Five Great Armies of the World

A TROOP
6th CAVALRY, U.S.A.

A TROOP
12th LANCERS, ENGLAND,
(Prince of Wales Regiment).

A TROOP
1st CARDE UHLAN REG'T,
"Potsdamer Reds," of His Majesty King Wilhelm II., German Emperor.

A TROOP
FRENCH CUIRASSEURS,
(Garde Republicaine).

A TROOP
RUSSIAN COSSACKS,
(From the Caucasus).

In a GRAND MILITARY TOURNAMENT, illustrating COMPANY, BATTALION and REGIMENTAL DRILL, with SABRE, LANCE and CARBINE, concluding with a

Monster Musical Ride at Full Gallop.

An Object Lesson to Every Military Man in America.

450 HORSES

OF ALL COUNTRIES.

The Greatest Equestrian Exhibition of the Century.

All under the direct personal supervision of

COL. W. F. CODY (BUFFALO BILL),
President.

MR. NATE SALSBURY,
Vice-President and Manager.

JOHN M. BURKE
General Manager.

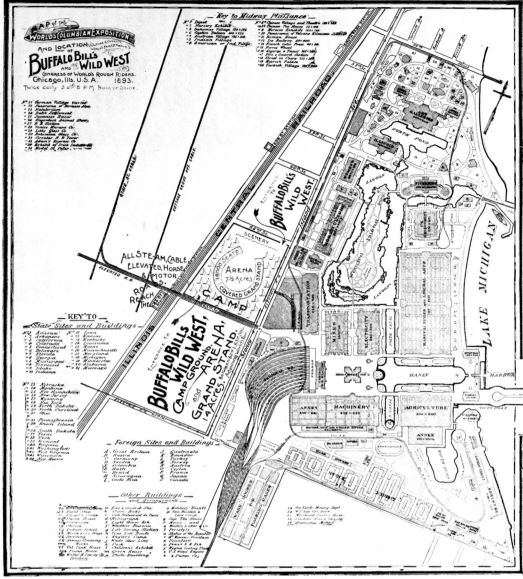

REMEMBER THE LOCATION---62D AND 63D STS.
ADJOINING WORLD'S FAIR GROUNDS.

TWO PERFORMANCES DAILY, 3 AND 8 P. M., RAIN OR SHINE.

Above:
Map of the 1893 Chicago World's Fair
Courtesy The Denver Public Library, Western History Department, Colorado

Left:
Ruby pressed crystal souvenirs of the Wild West show at the World's Fair
Collection: Buffalo Bill Historical Center, Cody, Wyoming

Above:
Buck Taylor, "King of the Cowboys,"
circa 1890
*Courtesy Buffalo Bill Historical Center,
Cody, Wyoming*

Below:
Poster
An American *circa* 1894
Printer: A. Hoen & Co., Baltimore,
Maryland
99 x 69 cm. (39 x 27 in.)
*Collection: Buffalo Bill Historical Center,
Cody, Wyoming*

The Wild West show, for the most part, was there to evoke the rough frontier past. Its function was nostalgic, almost elegiac—an appropriate mood for the year that saw Turner's famous announcement of the frontier's final closure. Its featured act was the climactic reenactment of Custer's Last Stand, the catastrophe that represented the simultaneous end of both the Indian's wilderness and the white man's wild frontier. The show's major star, Buck Taylor—"King of the Cowboys"—seems to have starred as Custer. After the melee Cody himself would appear amid the carnage, the tent lights would dim, and an illuminated screen would project the words "TOO LATE" above the stricken field and the solemn pose of Custer's would-be "rescuer." To this fantastic scene Cody brought the usual battery of authentications: publicity emphasizing Mrs. Custer's approval of the scene and assertions by army officers of its accuracy, appearances by original participants including 7th Cavalry troopers and Rain-in-the-Face. "Custer" was riding the war horse of Sitting Bull; in fact, the animal had been given to the chief as a gift when he was with the Wild West show, and Cody had reclaimed it after Wounded Knee. Cody's own recent bout with history on the eve of Wounded Knee was recalled by the use of the horse, by the publicity, and by the replica of Sitting Bull's cabin which the show displayed, and in which Cody conferred with Rain-in-the-Face. The Indian appears in the program as "The Former Foe—Present Friend, the American"; and the mood of white-Indian reconciliation is carried through by descriptions in journalistic publicity of friendly meetings between 7th Cavalry veterans of Little Big Horn and Wounded Knee and Sioux Indians in the Wild West show. Buffalo Bill here appears as the mediating figure in a scene reminiscent of those

blue-and-gray reconciliations of Civil War enemies; the Indian wars, like the Civil War, are seen to have ended in a heroic unification through violence, and to have provided a common *national* mythology of the vanished heroic past.[10]

However, the 1893 show was not all elegy. It included new elements that spoke more to the present and future. The most important of these was the addition of the "Congress of Rough Riders of the World"— indeed, the name of the show was changed to "Buffalo Bill's Wild West and Congress of Rough Riders of the World." The "rough rider" soubriquet had initially been used during the European tour, to characterize the American horseman. Now it was applied to a corps of foreign horsemen drawn from European military units and from the primitive horsemen in areas imperialized by the European powers. The Rough Riders opened the show with a "Grand Review," and various combinations of them raced and did equestrian tricks between the "Wild West" scenes. There was a "Horse Race between a Cowboy, a Cossack, a Mexican, an Arab, and an Indian, on Spanish-Mexican, Broncho,

Russian, Indian and Arabian horses." Each race or nationality rode its characteristic breed of hors and wore native costume. The different "natives" displayed their "sports and pastimes." The European horsemen represented elite military units, and their character as "regular army" representatives was repeatedly emphasized. One major part of the program was devoted to "Military Evolutions by a Company of the 6t Cavalry of the United States Army; Company of the First Guard Uhlan Regiment of His Majesty King William II, German Emperor, popularly known as the 'Potsdamer Reds'; a Company of French Chasseurs (Chasseurs à Cheval de Garde Republique Française); and Company of the 12th Lancers (Prince of Wales' Regiment) of the British Army." At the beginning and end of the show, these Rough Rider paraded, with Buffalo Bill at the head of the entire body, imperial soldiers and native "savages" alike.[11]

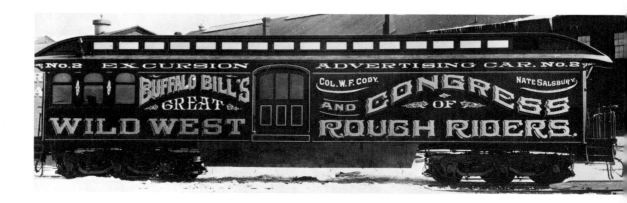

left:
Frederic Remington
Buffalo Bill in the Spotlight n.d.
oil on canvas
69.2 x 101.6 cm. (27¼ x 40 in.)
Collection: Buffalo Bill Historical Center,
Cody, Wyoming

facing page, bottom:
Special trains carried all the Wild West's
equipment, performers and animals.
Courtesy The Denver Public Library,
Western History Department, Colorado

below:
Buffalo Bill and the Wild West cast
Courtesy Wyoming State Library and
Archives, Cheyenne

The Rough Riders element in the show had an American precedent in the performances of special drill teams and zouave units that had been popular even before the Civil War. But Buffalo Bill's Rough Riders were professionals, not amateurs; and the context in which he placed them gave their appearance special meaning. He was creating a visual parallelism between the imperialism of Europe and of the United States—the 6th Cavalry with the Chasseurs, Indians with Arabs. And leading the whole "Congress" of imperial and native riders is the American frontier hero, "the King of them all," as General Carr had called him. In the context of the Columbian Exposition, and in the context of a show illustrating American progress by a ritual reenactment of the myth of the frontier, this display speaks of an extension of frontier symbolism into a new phase of expansion— expansion overseas, in an industrial and imperialist mode. If one cared to interpret the symbolism of the Rough Riders parade, it seemed to say that the spirit that conquered the West would ultimately place America at the head of a world order, in which each of the races would be bound to the other as

soldiers to the regiment or as native scouts to regular troops.

The Rough Rider theme is distinctly both militaristic and imperialist, and both of these elements figure in the expanded text of the program. An article by Colonel T.A. Dodge is quoted, which asserts that American cavalry will be the "pattern of the cavalry of the future," in a world characterized by struggle between civilized and savage races for mastery of Africa and Asia. There are references in the account of the European tour of the Wild West show to the prospect for a renewed European war over Alsace-Lorraine; a picture of Wounded Knee is used to illustrate the consequences that must follow such a calamity. Buffalo Bill's attempts to avert that massacre are cited as a model for the course of arbitration and mediation which, the program says, is the American government's suggestion for resolving such disputes. The leader of the Congress of Rough Riders thus appears to represent the American response to the major issues of international politics.[12]

The programs also contained explicit invocations to imperialist and Social Darwinist ideology. A new section on the Indian is frank about linking the history of white-Indian warfare

to Americans' pursuit of "the Anglo-Saxon's commercial necessities"; and while it pays tribute to the Indians' "better qualities" and treats their resistance with a chivalric respect, it asserts that "the inevitable law of the *survival of the fittest*" must determine the right to control "nature's cornucopia."[13]

David A. Curtis, writing in the *Criterion* in 1899, noted that the show's chief effect was to arouse "the ineradicable trace of savage instinct" that remains even in the most refined of civilized creatures— "kid gloves are strained over clenched fists." He found only one thing lacking—"that this latter day fighting is not real."[14] This lack, as we shall see, was in some measure compensated by the closer engagement of Buffalo Bill and the show with new imperial adventures overseas.

The Wild West thus moved from reenactment of the myth of the frontier to engagement with the making of the mythology of imperialism. It grounded its Social Darwinism and imperialism, ideologically and visually, in the symbolism of the frontier, and found

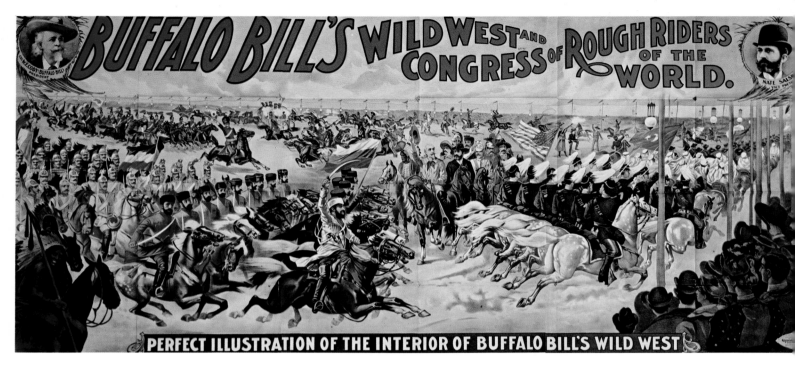

Above:
Poster
Perfect Illustration of the Interior of Buffalo Bill's Wild West
1896
Printer: Courier Lithographic Co.,
Buffalo, New York
6-sheet: 137 x 356 cm. (54 x 120 in.)
Collection: The Denver Public Library,
Western History Department, Colorado

Right:
Poster
Je Viens 1905
I am Coming
Printer: Weiners, Paris.
76 x 102 cm. (30 x 40 in.)
Collection: Buffalo Bill Historical Center,
Cody, Wyoming

in that symbolism prophecies and justifications for the assumption of world power by the United States, and for a new spirit of deliberate militarism. Its "Last Stand" was a grand and tragic farewell to the old frontier; its Rough Rider pageant a blithe and egotistical anticipation of the new.

Succeeding seasons amplified and developed this symbolism. The military exercise or battle reenactment and the concluding pageant of the Rough Riders of the World entered into the Wild West formula, occupying the same mythic space as the stagecoach attack, the settlers' cabin, the cowboy fun, the gunfight and the buffalo hunt. But unlike those elements, the military acts remained open to new input from ongoing historical events. In 1898, for example, the popular fever over the coming war with Spain led Cody to add to his Rough Riders representatives of the Cuban guerrillas and the Hawaiian islanders. A new version of "Custer's Last Fight" was mounted, as a reminder of the glory and the danger of America's just-closed domestic frontier. In the following year, the successful conclusion of the war was reflected in the substitution of Roosevelt's charge at San Juan Hill for the "Last Fight" as the climax of the show. Filipinos were now added to the Rough Riders, and audience reaction to them reflected shifts in

the public's attitude toward the new imperial adventure in the Philippines. The Filipinos were first cheered with the Cubans, then hissed when the "Insurrection" began. Finally, they were presented as Asian versions of the Apache scouts who had assisted in the suppression of Geronimo, and in this disguise were once again accepted by the public.

Above:
Poster
Ambrose Park, South Brooklyn 1894
Printer: Springer Lithographic Co., New York
71 x 107 cm. (28 x 42 in.)
Collection: Buffalo Bill Historical Center, Cody, Wyoming

Below:
Poster
A Squad of Genuine Cuban Insurgents 1898
Printer: Courier Lithographic Co., Buffalo, New York
71 x 107 cm. (28 x 42 in.)
Collection: Library of Congress, Washington, D.C.

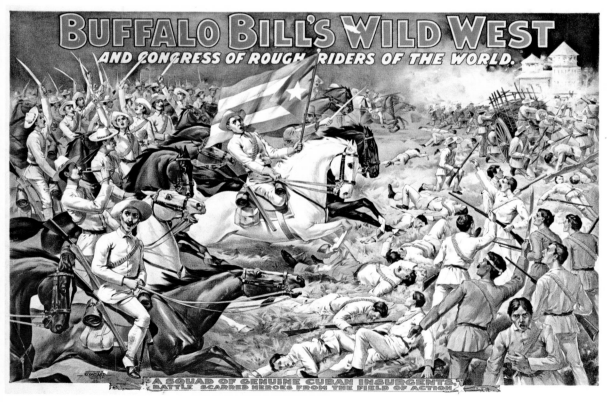

Above:
A Wild West stagehand operates an early floodlight.
Courtesy The Denver Public Library, Western History Department, Colorado

Left:
An advertisment for the Wild West show from *The Brooklyn Eagle* of April 11, 1897
Courtesy The Brooklyn Public Library, New York

Below:
The Wild West show's camp barber shop
Courtesy The Denver Public Library, Western History Department, Colorado

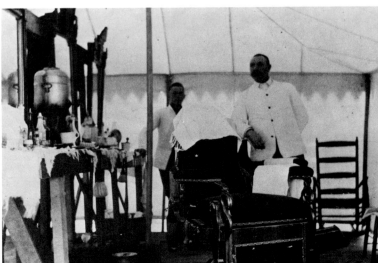

AMUSEMENTS. | AMUSEMENTS.

TWO WEEKS ONLY, BEGINNING TO-MORROW, APRIL 12.

AMBROSE PARK.
SOUTH BROOKLYN. Adjoining 39th Street Ferry,

37th Street and Third Avenue.
5th Ave "L" Direct to Park.
All Brooklyn City and Nassau
Electric Lines Transfer Direct to Park.

Renovated, Revived, Rehabilitated for the

TRIUMPHANT RETURN OF BROOKLYN'S OWN FAVORITE!
To the Park Designed, Constructed and Maintained as the Home of the Most Marvelous Amusement of
the Century, after a Tour of Two Seasons, which took it into Over 300 of the Principal Cities of
the United States, and Caused Brooklyn's Verdict to be Unanimously Endorsed.

BUFFALO BILL'S WILD WEST
AND CONGRESS OF ROUGH RIDERS OF THE WORLD.
AMERICA'S NATIONAL AMUSEMENT GLORY.
NEW IN MANY DETAILS, AND THE EQUESTRIAN CONGRESS BROUGHT STRICTLY UP-TO-
DATE, BY THE ADDITION OF IMPORTANT AND NUMEROUS FEATURES.
REALISTIC REVIEW OF

Romance and Reality

The One and Only

EXHIBITION

Which all Europe and America
have indorsed as

THE REAL THING!
No Tinsel. No Tinkling.
No Imitation About It.

ALL GENUINE,

All True, All Honest!

REVIVAL
OF
AMERICAN HISTORY MAKING
BY
SURVIVING PIONEERS
Who Created Western States.

HEREDITARY ENEMIES UNITED
In Showing the World the
Victory of Peace.

The Indian and the White Man
And all the World's
HEROIC HORSEMEN.

SOLITARY, UNIQUE--THE LAST OF ITS KIND.
100 Indian Warriors.

Ogallalla, Brule, Uncapappa, Sioux, Cheyenne and Arapahoe Tribes.

50 AMERICAN COWBOYS.	25 BEDOUIN ARABS.
30 MEXICAN VAQUEROS AND RURALIES.	20 RUSSIAN COSSACKS OF THE CAUCASUS.
50 WESTERN FRONTIERSMEN, MARKSMEN, ETC.	30 SOUTH AMERICAN GUACHOS.

MAGYAR GYPSY CHICOS from the Wild Steppes of Hungary. Never Before Seen
in America.

Detachment of Veteran United States Cavalry.

Batteries of Uncle Sam's Artillery.

ROYAL IRISH-ENGLISH LANCERS, GERMAN CUIRASSIERS. PETIT CORPS
D'ARMEE OF MOUNTED MILITARY.
ALL UNDER COMMAND OF

Col. W. F. CODY--Buffalo Bill
Who Will Positively Take Part in Both the Afternoon and Evening Exhibitions in
Person.

Miss ANNIE OAKLEY - - JOHNNY BAKER
The Peerless Lady Wing Shot. | The Skilled Shooting Expert.

The Only Herd of Buffalo on Exhibition.
NEXT MONDAY MORNING AT 9 O'CLOCK
The Cavalcade of all Nations Forming
THE GRAND FREE STREET PARADE
Will Leave Ambrose Park and Move Over the Following Route:

Ambrose Park to Fourth av, to Third st, to Sixth av, across Flatbush av, to St. Marks
av, to Bedford av, to Lafayette av, to Schermerhorn st, to Smith st, to Willoughby st, to
Court st, to Hamilton av, to Third av, to Camp at Ambrose Park.

TWO EXHIBITIONS DAILY, RAIN OR SHINE.
EVERY AFTERNOON AT 2 O'CLOCK. | EVERY NIGHT AT 8 O'CLOCK.
DOORS OPEN ONE HOUR EARLIER.

Cody took an active part in promoting the war, through the Wild West show and apart from it. He spoke in public in favor of intervention, and on the outbreak of hostilities offered to raise thirty thousand Indians to drive the Spaniards from Cuba, with a Sioux chief and the son of Geronimo as his assistants. Failing in this design, he contributed to General Miles the famous horse he had given to Sitting Bull, and later used in the "Last Fight" reenactment—a talismanic object that took the Wild West to war. But the most famous contribution of the show was the soubriquet "Rough Riders" adopted by Theodore Roosevelt's 1st Volunteer Cavalry. Roosevelt and Cody apparently disagreed about the source of the nickname, but Buffalo Bill was most generous in accepting Roosevelt into the company of frontier heroes. Issues of *The Rough Rider,* a magazine that

Cover of a 1905 French edition of
The Rough Rider
Collection: Buffalo Bill Historical Center,
Cody, Wyoming

The military camp at the Wild West show, Ambrose Park, South Brooklyn, 1897
Courtesy The Denver Public Library, Western History Department, Colorado

promoted the show, linked the battle of San Juan Hill with the Last Stand; and one cover showed Roosevelt and Cody together as "Men who have Led the Rough Riders of the World in Civic and Military Conquests."[16]

As the Wild West show entered the twentieth century, the centerpiece reenactments became more militaristic and imperialistic and more directly referential to contemporary history, while the "Western" acts remained the same. In 1901—02, San Juan Hill was replaced by the latest imperial combat, "The Battle of Tien-Tsin," reenacting the capture of that city

from the Chinese "Boxers." In 1903 San Juan Hill was brought back for an encore (the Philippine War having ended the previous year). In 1905, with the lull in such adventures, the "Last Fight" returned. This temporary reversion to Wild West materials continued in 1908 with the addition of the "Battle of Summit Springs" (an Indian battle from Cody's career) and "The Great Train Hold-Up and Bandit Hunters of the Union Pacific." The latter was both a typical Wild West act and a reenactment of an event that had occurred a few years before—and which had already been celebrated in the early Western movie The

Great Train Robbery (1903). Thus the trend toward contemporary reference continued, and eventually transformed the character of the show.[17]

The contextual rationale established by the printed program was altered to accommodate the show's new sense of itself. The 1907 program offers an essay on "Scouts Who Led to Empire," which sees the imperial destiny as inherent in the origins of America and of the frontier, and the "scout" as the necessary hero through whom that destiny is realized. The writer reaches back past the "scouts" traditionally linked with Buffalo Bill (Boone, Crockett,

Carson and Fremont), and establishes a more venerable ancestry in the figures of Columbus, Benjamin Church (hero of King Philip's War) and George Washington. Buffalo Bill appears in this history as the last exponent of the old type of frontier scout; and his career looks forward to that of Theodore Roosevelt, an Easterner who was "by nature imbued with the spirit of the Scout," and who carried the values acquired on the frontier to the very center of public life and international affairs.[18]

In 1908 the Wild West merged with Pawnee Bill's Far East, and the

Above:
The two Bills, Pawnee Bill (Gordon W. Lillie) and Buffalo Bill (William F. Cody), in 1908
Courtesy The Denver Public Library, Western History Department, Colorado

Right, above:
Poster
The Rescue at Pekin 1901
Printer: Enquirer Job Printing Co., Cincinnati, Ohio
9-sheet: 212 x 316 cm. (83 x 123½ in.)
Collection: Circus World Museum of Baraboo, Wisconsin

Right:
Poster
The Great Train Hold-Up 1907
Printer: Courier Lithographic Co., Buffalo, New York
12-sheet: 271 x 400 cm. (106 x 156 in.)
Collection: Buffalo Bill Historical Center, Cody, Wyoming

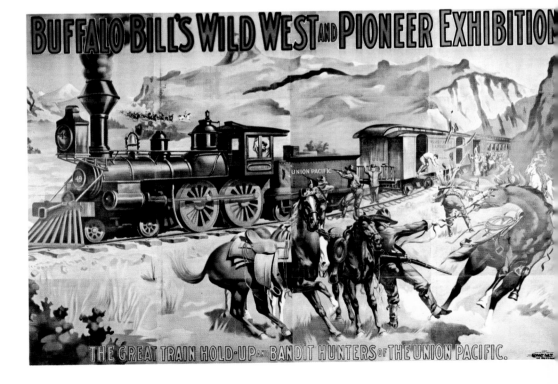

juxtaposition of Oriental and Wild West frontiers was presented in its most elaborate form. Both hemispheres were now comprehended in the mythic space of the Wild West. The "ethnological displays" offered "savages" from among the "pathetic" remnants of the Vanishing American and the "little brown men of the Orient." Rossi's Musical Elephants joined the bucking broncos; and the "Battle of Summit Springs" contrasted symmetrically with the elaborate pageant called "A Dream of the Orient." While the show declined financially, and Cody's management grip loosened in a series of partnerships, it continued to strain for relevance and connection. In 1916, on the eve of Cody's death, the theme of the combined Wild West 101 Ranch Show was "Preparedness" for American entrance into the First World War.[19]

The ultimate financial failure of Buffalo Bill's Wild West must not obscure its unparalleled success as a mythmaking enterprise. The Wild West show was the vehicle through which the symbolism of the frontier mythology was communicated to new generations of Americans— and Europeans—living in a "post-frontier" metropolitan society. The period of its European triumphs coincided with the period of massive immigration to America; and the Wild West, as many immigrants testified, was the source of some of their most vivid anticipatory images of the new land. The show was the source of images, staging techniques and personnel for the major medium that replaced it—the Western movie. And it communicated to its successor genre the interpretive linkage between mythologized past and contemporary event.

Nothing revealed Cody's skill and success as a mythmaker better than his manner of leaving the stage.

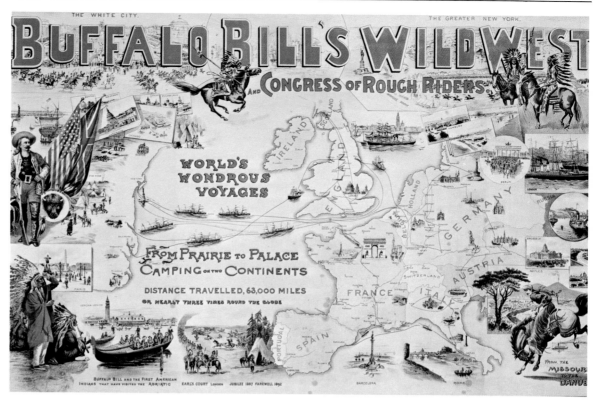

Above:
Poster
World's Wondrous Voyages 1894
Printer: A. Hoen & Co., Baltimore, Maryland
74 x 105 cm. (29 x 41½ in.)
Collection: Buffalo Bill Historical Center, Cody, Wyoming

Left:
Poster
The Farewell Shot 1910
Printer: Russell & Morgan Printing Co., Cincinnati, Ohio
104 x 71 cm. (41 x 28 in.)
Collection: Buffalo Bill Historical Center, Cody, Wyoming

Bottom, left:
Cody in 1907
Courtesy Buffalo Bill Historical Center, Cody, Wyoming

Below:
Two tickets for Buffalo Bill's Wild West and Pawnee Bill's Far East
Collection: Buffalo Bill Historical Center, Cody, Wyoming

His last years were marked by a seemingly endless cycle of "Farewell Performances." Despite the declining popularity of the now-hackneyed acts, affection and nostalgia for Buffalo Bill himself remained an exploitable commodity. There were, of course, strong financial motives behind these repeated farewells, and egotistical ones as well—the old trouper was reluctant to leave the stage.[20] But they also reveal the startling fact that the nostalgia for the vanishing "real frontier," which had been the show's original premise, had given way to a new form of the emotion: nostalgia not for the reality but for the myth—not for the frontier as it really was, but for "Buffalo Bill's Wild West."

Right:
Buffalo Bill on his favorite white horse, Isham, *circa* 1910
Courtesy Buffalo Bill Historical Center, Cody, Wyoming

Below:
"The Triumph of the West," a cartoon from the December 15, 1887 issue of *Life*

Research for this essay was supported by grants from the Rockefeller Foundation and the National Endowment for the Humanities, a Federal agency in Washington, D.C.

1.   See *America's Frontier Heritage* (New York, 1966) and *Frederick Jackson Turner: Historian, Scholar, Teacher* (New York, 1973), both by Ray Allen Billington; Henry Nash Smith, *Virgin Land: The American West as Symbol and Myth* (New York, 1950); and Richard Slotkin, *Regeneration Through Violence: The Mythology of the American Frontier, 1600-1860* (Middletown, CT, 1973).

2.   Don Russell, *The Lives and Legends of Buffalo Bill* (Norman: University of Oklahoma Press, 1960), pp. 265-84, 386-415. Prentiss Ingraham, *Adventures of Buffalo Bill from Boyhood to Manhood,* Beadle's Boy's Library no. 1 (New York, 1881) is reprinted in E. Bleiler, ed., *Eight Dime Novels* (New York, 1968). *Buffalo Bill and the Nihilists* (New York, 1910) is in the Western Americana Collection, Beinecke Library, Yale University, New Haven, CT. On the "last" theme, see Helen Cody Wetmore, *Last of the Great Scouts*

(Buffalo Bill), Afterword by Zane Grey (New York, 1918), particularly pp. 321-33. Grey says Cody thought of himself as a railroad builder rather than as a hunter.

3.   G. Edward White, *The Eastern Establishment and the Western Experience: The West of Frederic Remington, Theodore Roosevelt and Owen Wister* (New Haven, CT, 1968), p. 141.

4.   The best biography of Cody is Don Russell's *The Lives and Legends of Buffalo Bill* (see footnote 2) and is used for all biographical information cited below.

5.   Russell, *Lives and Legends,* chap. 25; Stanley Vestal, *Sitting Bull: Champion of the Sioux* (Norman, OK, 1932), chap. 36; and see footnote 10.

6.   The best account of the Wild West is Don Russell, *The Wild West: A History of Wild West Shows* (Fort Worth, TX, 1961), pp. 1-42. See also Russell, *Lives and Legends,* pp. 285-323. A useful supplement to Russell is Henry Blackman Sell and Victor Weybright, *Buffalo Bill and the Wild West* (New York: Oxford University Press, 1955).

7.   John M. Burke, "Salutatory," *Buffalo Bill's Wild West,* 1886 and 1887. All citations from Wild West programs are from copies in the Western History Department, Denver Public Library, CO. I am extremely grateful to Mrs. Eleanor M. Gehres and the library staff for their assistance.

8.   *Buffalo Bill's Wild West,* 1887. The "Programme" lists the acts or "Epochs" and briefly describes the action in each.

9.   Brick Pomeroy quoted in "Hon. W. F. Cody—'Buffalo Bill' "—a biographical sketch that included paragraphs on Cody as "A Legislator" and "As an Educator," the latter which contains the quote. The sketch and its

appendices appear virtually unchanged in most programs. See *Buffalo Bill's Wild West,* 1886 for the first version; also the programs of 1887 and 1893. The encomia from Cody's former commanders appeared in different forms, although the letters of commendation cited were always the same, and Carr's statement that Cody is "the King of them all" was always given special emphasis. See "Letters of Commendation from Prominent Military Men," *Buffalo Bill's Wild West,* 1886; and "A Record—Two Continents," *Buffalo Bill's Wild West,* 1887, which adds letters from European and American notables about the value of Cody's show.

10.   Publicity surrounding the 1893 appearance of the Wild West alongside the Columbian Exposition is collected in Cody Scrapbooks, vol. 2, particularly pp. 3, 8, 12, 21, 35, 37, 97-100, 102-107, at the Denver Public Library.

11.   "Programme" and "Salutatory," *Buffalo Bill's Wild West,* 1893, pp. 2,4. "American Rough Riders" are referred to in "Programme," *Buffalo Bill's Wild West,* 1887. Also see Russell, *Lives and Legends,* pp. 370-85, and Russell, *Wild West,* pp. 61-72.

12.   *Buffalo Bill's Wild West,* 1893. Dodge is quoted on p. 36; an extended section dealing with Cody, the Ghost Dance and Wounded Knee (with supporting documents and commendations) appears on pp. 32-6, 38-45, 49-53; and the Alsace-Lorraine material appears in the account of the European tour, pp. 60-1.

13.   *Buffalo Bill's Wild West,* 1893, p. 62.

14.   David A. Curtis, "The Wild West and What It Lacks," Cody Scrapbooks, vol. 7, p. 183.

15.   See *Buffalo Bill's Wild West,* 1898, 189? 1900; and Cody Scrapbooks, vol. 7, pp. iii, vi? xx, xxiv-v, 54-5, 65, 69, 73, 95, 97, 104, 10? for reactions to Spanish-American War elements in the show and Cody as "an avow? expansionist" in regard to the Philippines. Cody said that his support of the war was simply patriotic—his "heart" was not really " it." (Russell, *Lives and Legends,* p. 417.)

16.   Cody's offer to raise thirty thousand Indians was made in an interview with the Ne? York *World* in April, 1898 (Cody Scrapbooks vol. 7, front cover). An account of the peculia? history of the gift horse and its use by Sitting Bull, Cody and General Miles is given in Stanley Vestal, *Sitting Bull: Champion of the Sioux* (Norman, OK, 1932), pp. 250-51, 255-56, and chap. 36, and Russell, *Lives and Legends,* p. 363. For the Cody-Roosevelt controversy about the name of the regiment see *Buffalo Bill's Wild West,* 1899, p. 36; the San Juan Hill battle and the reenactment are described on pp. 32-6. *The Rough Rider* 1, n? 1 (1899), p. 12 refers to San Juan Hill in the context of Custer's Indian fights; the cover of *The Rough Rider* 3, no. 4 (1901) shows Roosevelt, Cody and Boer War horsemen Joubert and Baden-Powell, with the story "Men Who Have Led the Rough Riders of the World" on p. 2. Copies are in the Denver Public Library, CO.

17.   *Buffalo Bill's Wild West,* 1899, 1900, 1901, 1902, 1904, 1905, 1907, 1908. Russe? *Wild West,* p. 62.

18.   "Scouts Who Led to Empire," *Buffalo Bill's Wild West,* 1907.

19.   *Buffalo Bill's Wild West,* 1909, 1916. Jack Rennert, *100 Posters of Buffalo Bill's Wi? West* (New York, 1976), p. 93.

20.   Rennert, *100 Posters,* pp. 63, 108-09, 111; Russell, *Lives and Legends,* pp. 439-72.

Buffalo Bill and the Wild West

The Indians

Vine Deloria, Jr.

*University of Arizona
Tucson*

In the mind of the American public, Buffalo Bill is perceived as a showman, buffalo hunter and Indian fighter. The popular media has fostered this perception, vividly confirming his multifaceted identity as the impresario championing Annie Oakley; as the buffalo hunter skilled in marksmanship and horsemanship; and as the last of the great scouts, courageously leading the U.S. Cavalry on missions against the Plains Indians. In each case, Cody has been made to appear either shameless or noble, depending upon the attitude or thoroughness of those presenting the information.

Aware of the steadily rising revisionist concern for the history and current portrayal of the American Indian, we invited Vine Deloria, political scientist and author of *Custer Died for Your Sins,* to prepare an essay on the relationship of Buffalo Bill to the Indians. He has shared with us his sense of how Native Americans might feel today towards the "old Indian fighter." [DHK]

Digging beneath the massive number of legends and myths that surround Buffalo Bill to determine his actual relationship with the Indians is a singularly difficult task. So entrenched are the stories recounting some of his exploits that his many fans often insist that everything reported must have some kernel of truth. In fact, the old Plainsman, were he here today to

correct the historical record, might well be hard put to correlate legend and history himself. The uncritical posture adopted by many Western buffs can sometimes make it appear that Cody personified certain attributes of the last century which, in retrospect, we feel were destructive of the best parts of Western America—the Indians and the buffalo. The mass of material

Right:
Photographs by Edward S. Curtis (1868—1952): top, *Sioux Camp;* center, *Atsina Warriors*
Collection: The Denver Public Library, Western History Department, Colorado

Right, bottom:
Buffalo Bill with Sioux, Pawnee and Crow scouts
Courtesy Buffalo Bill Historical Center, Cody, Wyoming

Left, top:
William T. Hornaday's 1889 map of the
extermination of the buffalo
Collection: The Amon Carter Museum
Western Art, Fort Worth, Texas

Left, bottom:
Martin S. Garretson
The End, 1883 1913
Pen and ink on paper
41.3 x 63.2 cm. (16¼ x 24⅞ in.)
Collection: William S. Reese, New
Haven, Connecticut

Below:
"Pony Express" woodcut
Collection: Buffalo Bill Historical Center
Cody, Wyoming

Facing page, top:
Charles Marion Russell
Bringing Home the Spoils 1909
Oil on canvas
38.4 x 69.2 cm. (15⅛ x 27¼ in.)
Courtesy Buffalo Bill Historical Center
Cody, Wyoming

Facing page, center:
Indians in the Wild West show of 1894
Ambrose Park, South Brooklyn
Courtesy The Denver Public Library,
Western History Department, Colorado

Facing page, bottom:
Irving A. Bacon
Gen. Miles and Col. Cody on Winter
Campaign 1911
Oil on canvas
75.6 x 122.5 cm. (29¾ x 48¼ in.)
Collection: Buffalo Bill Historical Center
Cody, Wyoming

suggests however, that Cody regretted those occasions when he was viewed as an exterminator of either human or animal life.[1] To paint Buffalo Bill as the prototype of the hardline conservative is to refuse to confront the warmth of personality and to rely too much on the legend that has risen since Cody's time to enfold his memory.

Discussion of Buffalo Bill and the Indians falls naturally into three parts: his early life and activities as a scout and buffalo hunter; the Cody of the Wild West shows; and the fictional, primarily ahistorical character who is invoked to symbolize ideologies that he might not have approved had he been able to choose how he would be remembered. In dividing the discussion into these three categories we open up the possibility of separating fact from fiction, and allow the personality and the times to speak to us. We can, I believe, make some fair assumptions about the actual relationship of Cody and the Indians using this method of inquiry, and come to some basic conclusions that do justice to the man and the period of history he continues to represent.

□   □

The early, pre-show business Cody was not radically different from other young men growing up on the frontier and having survival as a first priority. One of the better Pony Express riders, Cody took his chances in traveling across lands that were not his or his country's while covering his routes. That Indians did chase and often kill Pony Express riders is historical fact, but no sense of personal animosity existed between the riders and the Indians. While Indians might take great pains to destroy telegraph wires and railroad tracks, systematic harrassment of Pony Express riders was not common. Perhaps the

The only known photograph of Buffalo Bill in Indian costume
Courtesy Buffalo Bill Historical Center, Cody, Wyoming

Indians saw in the young couriers the same strength and determination considered admirable in their own warrior traditions. In the treaty of Fort Laramie in 1851 the United States recognized the political right of the Northern Plains tribes to police their own lands and, until these lands were ceded, they properly belonged to, and were under the control of, these tribes; and intruders took their own risks.

Cody was also a scout for the Army and participated in a number of campaigns against the Indians—most notably against the Cheyennes who, during those years, seemed to have a genius for being in the wrong place at the wrong time and suffered grievously for their naiveté.[2] Scouting in those days was a tiresome and frustrating experience for knowledgeable Westerners. Army officers, often fresh from Civil War triumphs, represented the height of military arrogance and refused to believe that the Indians would or could mount a stubborn defense of their lands against white intruders. Cody was fortunate in working with Phil Sheridan and the 5th Cavalry rather than George Custer and the 7th Cavalry or the dreary procession of incompetents such as Fetterman and Grattan, who took themselves too seriously and paid a fearful price for their pride.[3] The business was rough, dirty and tedious and brought few moments of personal satisfaction. On the whole, civilian scouts did not display the arrogance and racism that infected the Army personalities and, measured against some of the other scouts who participated in the Indian campaigns, Cody seemed to transcend the petty egotism of the frontier. Indians respected him but, as often happened in the West, rarely understood that Buffalo Bill had been among those they encountered on the battlefield until long after the conflict. Since Cody was already a dime-novel

personality when he began scouting for the Army, his mere presence often ensured that spectacular exploits would be attributed to him. He probably contributed as much in morale to the Army of those days as he did in scouting and tracking skills.

The famous duel with Yellow Hand in the weeks following the Custer debacle is an instance of Cody's talent for attracting attention. An Army detachment encountered some Cheyennes barely a fortnight after the fight on the Little Big Horn and, assuming that all Indian bands still roving the Wyoming-Montana-Nebraska-Dakota wilderness region were hostile and had taken part in the fight in Montana, the Army initiated action against them. A number of men fired at a distant Indian who attracted attention because of his spectacular war bonnet. The Indian went down and Cody reached the body first and scalped the fallen man. The fervor of the moment, coupled with the newspaper reports' obvious effort to portray the incident as the "First Scalp for Custer," transformed a rather commonplace occurrence into a superhuman act by the West's most famous personality. Whether or not Cody's shot actually felled the Cheyenne warrior seems impossible to determine; Cody did, however, receive much favorable publicity for having accomplished this feat.

While life on the frontier provided many opportunities for earning a reputation as a fighting man, instances of spectacular individual accomplishments are rare indeed. Cody was never credited with a feat of skill comparable to the famous incident at Adobe Walls in which a frontiersman felled an Indian warrior with a single shot at a distance estimated at close to a mile.[4] In fact, Cody had no occasion to demonstrate unparalleled skill as a fighting man because of the circumstances in which he found

himself. Yet the consensus of repo; seems to be that Cody's bravery, scouting ability and marksmanship were better than most—rivaled by few other individuals. Cody's inna† ability to attract legend to himself provided sufficient opportunity to raise ordinary performance to the status of supernatural feat, and the combination seemed unbeatable and accepted throughout the West. Caught in a fight, Buffalo Bill gave good account of himself and other. elaborated on his accomplishment to provide us with legends.

During the Ghost Dance troubles Cody was asked to confer with Sitting Bull—who had traveled wi† him in the Wild West show half a decade before—and he would hav completed this mission had the government agent not prevented him from talking with the old medicine man. The following sprin when whites in Nebraska were stil fearful over the chances of war wi† the Sioux, Cody was serving as Brigadier General of Nebraska militia. He provided good morale, calm and seasoned experience, ar considerable wisdom in his service with the state troops, successfully avoiding further military confrontation. Had Cody possesse the fearsome and bloodthirsty personality which some dime nov implied, there would certainly hav been an ugly incident during his s† as commander of the Nebraska forces. A lesser figure might have used the opportunity to create his own Indian war—as did Colonel Chivington in 1864 while serving the Colorado militia under similar circumstances.[5] But the fact that s few incidents occurred during Cody's militia service is an indicat of his humanity.

When judged according to the prevailing standards of the times, Buffalo Bill's relationship with the Indians, absent the aura of show business, seems above average in

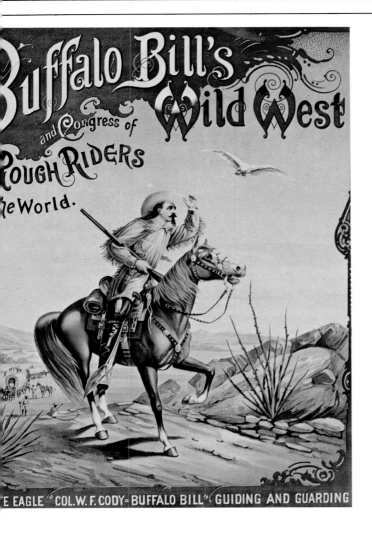

Above:
Posters
The White Eagle and The Red Fox
1893
Printer: A. Hoen & Co., Baltimore, Maryland
Each 73.6 x 55.9 cm. (29 x 22 in.)
Collection: Buffalo Bill Historical Center, Cody, Wyoming

Left:
The attack on Sand Creek: In the early morning of November 29, 1864, Colonel John Chivington led an attack on a village of Cheyennes and Arapahoes, living in peace under U.S. government protection (see American and white flags in center of village) at Sand Creek in Southeastern Colorado. Four to five hundred Indians were killed.
Courtesy Brown Brothers, Sterling, Pennsylvania

the positive human qualities of justice and fair play—exemplifying, and perhaps creating, the traditional code of the West as it was later articulated in books and movies. No strain of racial antagonism seems to have motivated Cody; his ethics and personal integrity appear solid and admirable.[6] When we ask whether this sense of dignity and personal integrity meant that Indians trusted Cody more than other whites they encountered, we have little evidence to argue either way. Few Indians had much contact with any particular frontiersman of Cody's era, so it is not surprising that we have so little indication of how Indians felt. Of frontier personalities who had a special relationship of trust with any particular group of Indians, perhaps only Sam Houston and Tom Jeffords seem to have succeeded, and the unique circumstances of these two cases make it impossible to draw any distinct comparison.[7] Considerably more individuals fell into the classification of "untrustworthy," but there is also, perhaps, a middle ground in which such figures as Buffalo Bill, Jim Bridger and General Crook were considered people who understood how Indians felt and dealt with some measure of justice in their relationships with the tribes.

One can argue that the omissions of Buffalo Bill's life illuminate his personal integrity far more than some of his deeds. Though he was an Army scout during the most intense period of conflict with the Indians, Cody did not participate in any treaty negotiations, nor did he ever consent to be used by the United States government to convince the Indians that they should cede lands, allow mining of them, adopt industry or railroads on them, agree to allot their lands and learn to live as farmers. At one time or another, nearly every Christian missionary, trapper, trader or freighter did allow himself to be used

Cody, circa 1915
Courtesy Buffalo Bill Memorial Museum, Golden, Colorado

Top:
Indians with the Wild West show: (from left) Black Hawk and his wife, Rocky Bear and Standing Bear
Courtesy The Denver Public Library, Western History Department, Colorado

Below:
The wedding of High Bear and Holy Blanket in the Wild West camp
Courtesy The Denver Public Library, Western History Department, Colorado

Above:
Women visitors with Sitting Bull (sixth from left, back row), backstage at the Wild West show, circa 1885
Courtesy The Denver Public Library, Western History Department, Colorado

Facing page:
Sitting Bull with Buffalo Bill
Courtesy The Denver Public Library, Western History Department, Colorado

s a negotiator of treaties or become involved in promises made by the government that everyone knew were doomed from the very start. Cody was no fool when it came to understanding government policy and his noted absence at the great treaty sessions indicates that he regarded his own personal integrity as beyond price. His record, where promises made to the Indians are concerned, is much stronger than that of such revered figures as Father DeSmet, Bishop Whipple or Bishop Hare, or a succession of American presidents.[8] We can conclude that he never knowingly placed himself in a position where he would have to lie to the Indians. This should be remembered in any appraisal of Buffalo Bill—because he certainly had the opportunities to do so had he taken that path.

☐   ☐

When we examine Buffalo Bill's show business career, events take on a different interpretation. Here he appears as a very positive person who earned and held the respect of the Sioux Indians. Numerous anecdotes recount acts of kindness attributed to Cody during the course of tours both here and in Europe. Luther Standing Bear, for example, who toured abroad with Buffalo Bill in 1905, cited an instance in which the cowboys gave the Indians the toughest mounts to ride during the performances in England. After complaining to Cody about the situation, Luther was astounded to see the cowboys mounting the unruly horses that very afternoon and, although Bill said nothing to anyone about the complaint, Standing Bear recalled that there was the slightest trace of a smile and a definite twinkle in Cody's eyes during the performance that day.[9]

Cody recruited Indians primarily from the Oglala Sioux bands at the Pine Ridge reservation in western South Dakota. His first major achievement was getting Sitting Bull to tour with him during the 1885 season. Sitting Bull had toured with Colonel Alvaren Allen the year before and the experience was very unsatisfactory. Allen neither accorded the old medicine man personal respect, nor did he use the Sioux leader as a major attraction of the show. Learning from this unpleasant experience, Sitting Bull, when invited by Cody to join the troupe, asked for fifty dollars a month and all the income that might be generated from having pictures taken of him.[10] Arizona John Burke recruited the Sioux medicine man for Cody, but it was Buffalo Bill who recognized immediately the Indian's drawing power and personal dignity, and gave him a positive role to play in the show. Rather than require Sitting Bull to participate in the mock battles and otherwise make a fool of himself, Buffalo Bill treated the old man as a distinct and noble personality. At an opportune time in the show Sitting Bull would be announced; he would ride impassively and nobly into the arena alone on a horse and for several moments be the sole attraction of the show. Rather than the fearful savage of pulp novels, Sitting Bull was seen as the charismatic statesman of an Indian nation and, like Cody's own image, this picture of Sitting Bull became imprinted in the minds of the audience.

Show business necessities probably dictated that Cody use Sitting Bull as the leader of the Indian riders in the mock battles with the cowboys, but doing so might have rubbed the old wounds grievously. It is almost impossible today to understand the courage of the old Sioux as day after day he rode alone into the arena to be booed and hissed as Custer's killer—aware, perhaps, that some disgruntled patron in the audience, seeking to avenge the popular general, might take a shot at him.

That such an incident did not occur is, I believe, testimony to Buffalo Bill's genius in emphasizing Sitting Bull's stature and humanity. His treatment of Sitting Bull was such that thoughts of revenge never went beyond the stage of hissing, and the audience undoubtedly felt that if the old scout had made friends with the Sioux medicine man, then they also could let bygones be bygones.

While in Canada during this tour, Cody took the initiative in explaining the Indian side of the story. He was quoted in a Toronto newspaper as saying that "In nine cases out ten when there is trouble between white men and Indians, it will be found that the white man is responsible. Indians expect a man to keep his word. They can't understand how a man can lie. Most of them would as soon cut off a leg as tell a lie." And later in that tour he remarked:

> The defeat of Custer was not a massacre. The Indians were being pursued by skilled fighters with orders to kill. For centuries they had been hounded from the Atlantic to the Pacific and back again. They had their wives and little ones to protect and they were fighting for their existence. With the end of Custer they considered that their greatest enemy had passed away. Sitting Bull was not the leader of the Sioux in that battle. He was a medicine man who played on their superstitions—their politician, their diplomat—who controlled their emotions through the power of his argument and the vehemence of his speech.[11]

Buffalo Bill's role in Canada was that

of an authority, not as the star of the show—who turned out to be Sitting Bull himself. When Sitting Bull left the show after the season, Buffalo Bill gave him a trick riding horse that he admired, and there seems to have been an unspoken but intuitive bond of friendship and respect between the men.

Other Oglala Sioux toured with Cody regularly. Among some of the more important personalities were Kicking Bear and Short Bull, who had been involved in the Ghost Dance; young Black Elk, who was stranded in Europe for a few years and left the show in time to arrive in South Dakota just before the Wounded Knee massacre—which he survived; Lone Bull; No Neck; Plenty Horses; Rocky Bear; Young-Man-Afraid-of-His-Horses; and Red Cloud's son, Jack Red Cloud. Because Cody was intent on showing the great variety of events and personalities that had produced the Western frontier, many of these Sioux were listed in the programs under other tribal affiliations so that the audience would believe Cody had recruited the most fearsome warriors of each tribe for his shows. Thus some of the Sioux chiefs were listed as chiefs of the Cheyenne and Arapaho tribes, although in fact they were almost all from the Pine Ridge reservation in South Dakota. But such fictions were a necessary part of show business and were not seen by the Indians as anything more than an effort to increase the excitement that the show engendered.[12] In any case, there would have been enormous problems had Cody actually recruited members of a variety of tribes; this tactic ensured the Indians of a good experience with the show.

Two very important points must be made with respect to the participation of Indians in the Wild West. First, Buffalo Bill's prestige enabled him to arrange for

individuals otherwise regarded as dangerous characters to leave the reservation and participate in his tours without alarming the Bureau of Indian Affairs—which in those days was liable to panic at any unexpected development among its Indian charges. Cody had Short Bull, Kicking Bear, Young-Man-Afraid-of-His-Horses and Sitting Bull with him on tour while they were still regarded by the Indian agents as major troublemakers in the Sioux tribe. Many Indian agents and Army officers would have preferred to see these characters in the stockade. Touring with Buffalo Bill probably saved some of the chiefs from undue pressure and persecution by the government at home.

Other than seeing that the Indian encampment was not disturbed by

BUFFALO BILL'S WILD WEST

HE-NU-KAW. (The first born.)

Facing page, top:
Red Cloud, Buffalo Bill and American Horse at Madison Square Garden, New York, 1886
Courtesy The Denver Public Library, Western History Department, Colorado

Facing page, center:
Chief Joseph and Buffalo Bill behind the scenes at the Wild West show, *circa* 1904
Courtesy The Denver Public Library, Western History Department, Colorado

Facing page, bottom:
Wild West show Indians playing ping-pong backstage
Courtesy The Denver Public Library, Western History Department, Colorado

Above:
Poster
Three Riders 1905
Printer: Chaix, Paris, France
76 x 105 cm. (30 x 41 in.)
Collection: Bibliothèque Nationale, Paris, France.
From 100 Posters of Buffalo Bill's Wild West by Jack Rennert, Copyright 1976 Darien House, Inc.

Right:
Red Cloud, Buffalo Bill and American Horse
Courtesy The Denver Public Library, Western History Department, Colorado

Far right:
Poster
He-Nu-Kaw. (The first born) 1881
Printer: W. J. Morgan & Co., Lithographers, Cleveland, Ohio
76.2 x 40.6 cm. (30 x 16 in.)
Collection: Buffalo Bill Historical Center, Cody, Wyoming

outsiders, Cody did not place any except normal restrictions on the Indians, and these rules would have applied to any Westerners unfamiliar with the big city during those years. Cody only wanted to ensure that his people would not be taken advantage of by swindlers. The fact that these Sioux leaders, each capable of inspiring and directing thousands of people, gave Cody no trouble whatsoever during the tours is further evidence of his fine relationship with them.

The second important point regarding the Indians and the Wild West concerns the Indians' status as performers. Much of the emphasis of the performance was on the Congress of Rough Riders, which represented some of the finest horsemen in the world: American military such as the Cavalry and Artillery, a contingent of Roosevelt's Rough Riders, cowboys, English Lancers, German Cuirassiers, Mexicans, Cossacks, Arabs, Cubans, Hawaiians, Filipinos and, of course, American Indians. Instead of degrading the Indians and classifying them as primitive savages, Cody elevated them to a status of equality with contigents from other nations. In so doing, he recognized and emphasized their ability as horsemen and warriors and stressed their patriotism in defending their home lands. This type of recognition meant a great deal to the Indians who were keenly aware that American public opinion often refused to admit the justice of their claims and motivations. Inclusion of

Indians in the Congress of Rough Riders provided a platform for diplaying natural ability that transcended racial and political antagonisms and, when contrasted with other contemporary attitudes toward Indians, represented one that was amazingly sophisticated and liberal.

The Wild West shows performed a very important function in the closing decades of the last century. Indian leaders were generally carted to Washington, kept enclosed in a hotel room until they were ushered in to see the President or the Secretary of the Interior, sternly admonished to sign the treaty or agreement that ceded large tracts of tribal lands, and then unceremoniously sent home to the reservations where immature, partially educated and generally inexperienced agents worked to undercut their dignity and authority. The Wild West shows—particularly Cody's troupe—offered a great deal

more. Touring with Buffalo Bill enabled a whole generation of Indians to learn about American society in a relatively non-threatening atmosphere. Although most of the chiefs had experienced a tremendous shock in being confined to the reservations, the Wild West served to give them confidence in themselves by emphasizing the nobilitiy of their most cherished exploits and memories.

Travel with the shows generally meant leaving the reservation for the better part of a year. Some Indians were afraid to leave their relatives for that long a period of time; deaths might occur and customary and ceremonial responsibilities might have to be postponed until they returned. Frontier conditions still existed in much of the West and a strong possibility existed—as evidenced by the Wounded Knee massacre of 1890—that Army troops might attack their tribes while

Indians were away on tour. Clearly, joining the Wild West was not an easy decision. But the freedom these Indians experienced with Buffalo Bill, and the chance to learn about the rest of the world, held sufficient appeal to lure many of the chiefs away from the reservation. As a transitional educational device wherein Indians were able to observe American society and draw their own conclusions, the Wild West

was worth more than every school built by the government on any of the reservations. Unlike the government programs, the Wild West treated the Indians as mature adults capable of making intelligent decisions and of contributing to an important enterprise. Knowledge o white society gained in tours with Cody stood many of the Indians in good stead in later years, and without this knowledge, the

Above:
Detail of a panoramic view of the Wild West cast, 1909, Brooklyn, New York
Courtesy Buffalo Bill Historical Center, Cody, Wyoming

Facing page, left:
Cody and Indians in Venice
Courtesy Buffalo Bill Historical Center, Cody, Wyoming

Below:
The 7th Cavalry destroys an Indian camp: a scene from *The Indian Wars,* a 1913 production of Essanay and Colonel W. F. Cody Historical Pictures, filmed at Pine Ridge, South Dakota
Courtesy Norman Alley Collection, California

government's exploitation of the Sioux during the period before the First World War might have been even more harsh.

☐   ☐

Buffalo Bill as literary legend and show business personality presents a much more difficult subject to examine. There is little doubt in anyone's mind that the dime novel used the Indian as the villain and relied heavily upon racial slurs and derogatory stereotypes to support most of the plots. Dime novels attributed evil and savage motives to the Indians so that the white hero would be seen in a favorable light. That many whites accepted these distortions as historical fact is unfortunate, but is also a testimony to the generally shallow intellectual capabilities of Americans that de Tocqueville had originally identified.[13] Like contemporary movies, television shows and novels, the authors of these fictional

pulp stories were generally Easterners who had never seen the West and who committed to paper fantasies and stereotypes that no self-respecting, experienced Westerner would have tolerated for a moment. Then, like today, the credibility of the story depended almost wholly on its popularity and commercial success—not upon any relationship to historical or geographical reality.

Once Cody became a character in this literature he was the victim of a public demand that proved nearly insatiable. Exploits that were technically impossible became commonplace in his literary existence. To deny his superhuman powers would have been to call down the wrath of a gullible public. So Cody was stuck with a public image that grew more reactionary yet abstractly sublime as the years passed. Frightened at the changes that large industry was making in their lives, Americans sought in

Cody and other mythical Western heroes assurance that frontier virtues were capable of transcending the determinism of historical and natural processes. This transformation of the Western hero from historical personage to a quasi-religious-political testimony to American values probably forced Cody to use the increasingly melodramatic plots in his shows. It also must have motivated him to attempt to film a reenactment of the Wounded Knee massacre on the very site where the slaughter occurred. The Sioux protested this effort quite vigorously but were finally cajoled into appearing by the old scout himself; this one act destroyed much of the good will that Cody had painstakingly earned over the decades. But the film was made in Cody's later years when his fortunes were declining precipitously, and can probably be attributed to his urgent desire to recapture his youth and popularity at a time when the public wanted to

forget Cody, Indians and the West, and enjoy the luxuries of modern life.

Some evidence exists that Cody became embarrassed at the legends attached to his name that credited him with both fictitious adventures and a racial hatred of Indians. Though cast as the hero, there was a great deal written in the dime novels that made Cody look ridiculous in the eyes of Westeners who knew the frontier and the Indians. When asked how many Indians he had killed—as if this score should be comparable to the number of buffalo he had killed or, in a modern context, the number of home runs a baseball player had hit—the old scout would frequently refuse to answer, replying only that he had never killed an Indian who was not trying to kill him.[14] This response was a polite and sophisticated way of saying that he had not killed any Indians for sport, did not approve the practice, and certainly did not consider the Indians enemies. So powerful was the legend that surrounded Cody that a frank answer would probably have been challenged by his many fans as being out of character for Buffalo Bill.

Even today, evaluating Cody and the Indians is a difficult problem because of the long heritage of dime novels and movies that have driven stereotypes deep into the collective American psyche. So entrenched is the legend of Buffalo Bill that the first question that arises regarding him is whether or not legend actually preceded him. When all the evidence is considered, Buffalo Bill seems to have been a kindly, decent person who treated everyone with dignity and respect. That his figure has become a vehicle for the continuation of discriminatory and derogatory images of Indians is tragic, and would probably have been disclaimed by Cody to intimate friends. He rarely disclaimed his legend, however, and this inability to distinguish fact from fiction in his own life probably qualifies Buffalo Bill as the first truly national show business personality—an entirely different kind of person than America had ever experienced before.

Since it is impossible to separate fact from fiction in the public perception of Buffalo Bill, the greatness of his personality and his strong sense of identity and integrity will probably never be understood. He was truly a man of his times, and today the West that he loved and represented is little more than an economic colony of the urban concentrations where Cody made his biggest impact. Buffalo Bill and the Indians spent their declining years in playacting a drama that had unfolded during their youth. Perhaps they realized, in the deepest sense, that even a caricature of their youth was preferable to a complete surrender to the homogenization that was overtaking American society.

Indians would prefer to leave these ghosts alone, but that is not the white man's way. Unable to capture the spirit of their own times, they insist on memorializing the past and collecting artifacts of former times—as if possessing implements of the past guaranteed present realities and gave them roots. Recognizing this altogether human dimension of the American psyche, Buffalo Bill wanted to be buried on a mountain overlooking Western lands. Perhaps he hoped that by remaining close to the plains he loved he might serve in death to remind us of the fundamental unity of people and land. This intuitive grasp of the meaning of human life was wholly Indian, and we like to think that in his heart of hearts, Buffalo Bill in death joined that closer human unity which the Western lands have always given to their sons and daughters.

Below:
Arthur Jule Goodman
King Edward VII at the Wild West 190
Watercolor
106.7 x 76.2 cm. (42 x 30 in.)
Collection: Buffalo Bill Historical Center Cody, Wyoming

Bottom:
The place where Buffalo Bill wanted to be buried, pointed out by guide, Ned Frost, who was with him when he placec stones at the spot near Cody, Wyoming *Courtesy Buffalo Bill Historical Center, Cody, Wyoming*

1. Richard J. Walsh, *The Making of Buffalo Bill* (New York: Bobbs-Merrill Company, 1928), p. 18. See also Henry Blackman Sell and Victor Weybright, *Buffalo Bill and the Wild West* (New York: Oxford University Press, 1955), p. 185.

2. The Cheyennes were at Sand Creek when Chivington attacked them, and the same band happened to be on the Washita River when Custer was looking for Indians to fight. The survivors of the Tall Bull and Black Kettle group arrived at the Little Big Horn in time for Custer's Last Stand.

3. Grattan invaded a Sioux camp with about a dozen men; Fetterman attacked an unknown number of Sioux out of sight of Fort Phil Kearney. See Dee Brown, *Bury My Heart at Wounded Knee* (New York: Holt, Rhinehart and Winston, 1971).

4. On July 1, 1874, Billy Dixon, one of the beseiged traders at Adobe Walls, used a Sharps buffalo rifle to hit an Indian warrior who was a stone's throw from a mile away from him. See Ralph K. Andrist, *The Long Death* (New York: Macmillan, 1964), p. 188.

5. Brown, *Wounded Knee*, chap. 4; Andrist, *The Long Death*, pp. 88-96.

6. Luther Standing Bear relates an incident in England when the manager of the dining hall at the hotel where the Wild West was staying tried to serve the Indians cold, leftover pancakes. Cody cornered the man and said "Look here, sir, You are trying to feed my Indians the leftover pancakes from the morning meal. I want you to understand, sir, that I will not stand for such treatment. My Indians are the principal feature of this show and they are the one people I will not allow to be misused or neglected. Hereafter see to it that they get just exactly what they want at meal time." (*My People the Sioux* [Boston: Houghton-Mifflin, 1928], pp. 260-61.)

7. Sam Houston is generally credited with protecting the Alabama-Coushatta Indians from the ire of the Texans so that they were the single remaining tribe left in Texas after the Indian wars—all the rest having been removed to Oklahoma. Tom Jeffords was the famous Indian agent who courageously protected the Apaches when most of Arizona Territory wished to conduct a war of extermination against them. The story of his relationship with the Apaches is well told in Elliott Arnold, *Blood Brother*, ed. Dale Nichols (New York: Hawthorn Books, 1947).

8. Bishop Whipple, Bishop Hare and Father DeSmet were all at one time or another participants in treaty negotiations and assured the tribes that the government would live up to its word. Hare, in fact, was enthusiastic about the General Allotment Act and used his influence to get the Sioux to accept it. But none of the promises these clerics made were ever kept; they apparently lost interest in ensuring that the government fulfilled its word to the Indians.

9. Luther Standing Bear, *My People the Sioux* (Boston: Houghton-Mifflin, 1928), pp. 264-65.

10. Henry Blackman Sell and Victor Weybright, *Buffalo Bill and the Wild West* (New York: Oxford University Press), p. 147.

11. Sell and Weybright, *Buffalo Bill and the Wild West*, pp. 147-48.

12. Don Russell, *The Wild West* (Fort Worth, TX: The Amon Carter Museum of Western Art, 1970), p. 72.

13. Alexis de Tocqueville, *Democracy in America* (New York: Doubleday Anchor Books, 1969), vol. 1, p. 56.

14. Sell and Weybright, *Buffalo Bill and the Wild West*, p. 185.

Buffalo Bill and the Wild West

The Cowboys

Howard R. Lamar

Yale University
New Haven, Connecticut

Although he worked in a wide variety of occupations, Buffalo Bill was never himself a cowboy—a hired hand employed to wrangle cattle. He made use of cowboys as important performers in his Wild West exhibitions, hired them to work on his ranches, and played a major role in popularizing the image of the cowboy as it is known today, particularly in Europe. As Howard Lamar points out, Cody's interpretation of the cowboy emphasized the individual spirit, energy, skill and self-confidence that characterize one of America's most enduring and popular figures. [DHK]

Left:
Poster
Annie Oakley/Johnnie Baker 1898
Printer: Enquirer Job Printing Co.,
Cincinnatti, Ohio
3-sheet: 210 x 105 cm. (82 x 41½ in.)
Collection: Circus World Museum of Baraboo, Wisconsin

Below:
James Walker
Vaqueros Roping Horses in a Corral 1887
Oil on canvas
60.9 x 101.6 cm. (24 x 40 in.)
Collection: The Thomas Gilcrease Institute of American History and Art, Tulsa, Oklahoma

For many years it has been the fashion to deride William F. Cody as a talented but egotistical showman whose Wild West productions exploited the American Indian, the frontier scout, the skills of "Little Miss Sure Shot" (Annie Oakley), and the cowboy. Such a judgment, while having some basis in fact, does not do justice to Cody's own remarkable career as a scout, guide and hunter on the frontier, nor does it show an understanding of Cody's uncanny sense of American popular history. Who else had the presence of mind or the gall to print the histories of Daniel Boone, David Crockett and Kit Carson along with his own autobiography? Least of all does this view suggest how much Cody contributed to the positive image of the cowboy, a figure that continues to symbolize the American character in the minds of people all over the world.[1]

William G. "Buck" Rainey has observed that "at the mention of 'cowboy,' a hundred different images are fashioned in the minds of as many different people." Cowboy, writes Rainey, could mean the hero of Wild West stories, rodeo performer, movie actor , singer, dude ranch wrangler, Wild West performer, Mexican vaquero in Texas, rough rider, bad man of the Plains and even Southwestern rancher. And then, of course, there is also the real cowboy who works on a ranch with real cattle.[2]

Don Russell, the Cody biographer, agrees with Joe B. Frantz and Julian E. Choate, Jr., authors of a major work on the cowboy, that there are three obvious "types": the historical, the fictional and the folkloric cowboy.[3] The historical cowboy, writes Russell, emerged about one hundred and fifteen years ago; the dime-novel cowboy appeared a bit later, in the 1870s; and the cowboy of folklore only emerged in this century.[4]

The origins of the American cowboy have been so romaticized that it is difficult to find agreement on exactly when he first appeared on the American scene. Colonial records suggest that mounted frontiersmen, often called rangers, rounded up wild or stray cattle from the pea vine marshes or other good grazing lands of the Atlantic seaboard and Appalachian frontier, and drove them to market. These drovers were often mere youths. Wild and funloving, they were certainly the prototypes of the men and boys who later participated in the long drives over the trails from Texas to the railheads of Kansas in the 1870s and 80s. In the seventeenth and eighteenth, as in the nineteenth centuries, the reasons for the drives were obvious: the cattle were a profitable product that could walk itself to market.[5]

Davy Crockett, while still a boy, was hired to drive cattle from Tennessee to Baltimore, where he and his teenaged companions were bilked of their wages by the dishonest owner of the herd.[6] After white settlers crossed the Appalachians, cattle herds could be found ahead of the line of settlement, and as early as the 1850s Illinois cattle raisers went "West" to Iowa or Missouri or other frontiers to purchase cattle for an Eastern market.

At the same time, cattle were so plentiful on the frontiers of the Old South that historians now assert the region was the first true home of the open range cattle industry.[7] To the west lay yet another cattle frontier, for the gaunt, horned Andalusian cattle introduced to Texas in the eighteenth century had multiplied by the 1850s to produce enormous herds. Even before the Civil War, Texas cattle were driven eastward to the New Orleans market.[8] In short, rangers, drovers or herdsmen had been a part of the moving frontier since the founding of the thirteen

colonies. Don Russell finds that the infamous Tory raiders who plagued the American frontier during the American Revolution were, in effect, cowboy ruffians.[9]

The person we identify today as the historic cowboy appeared, however, after the Civil War, when thousands of youths, ex-soldiers from the Confederate Army, and a lesser number of migrants from the North and Old Northwest, went west for a new start. Many were already familiar with cattle herding. They hired out to ranchers who were anxious to sell the millions of open range Texas cattle to customers wherever they might be—New Orleans, or north and east.

Once in Texas the new cowboy encountered an indigenous cowboy of sorts: the Mexican vaquero, whose striking outfit of tight trousers, silk sash, fancy vest, vast sombrero, and elaborate boots, saddles and spurs, was soon adopted—in part, at least—by many Anglo-American cowboys.[10] Even so, herding on the open range was not yet a glamorous life. Cowboys suffered injuries from falls, or drowned in swollen streams while attempting to drive cattle from one side to the other. They developed hernias or got kicked or stampeded. But the unattractiveness of the job didn't seem to discourage people. Indians and blacks also served as cowboys in the open range period. Black Americans, many of them ex-slaves, eventually made up one-seventh of the cowboy population.[11]

The economic breakthrough for the Texas cattlemen came in 1867 when Joseph G. McCoy blazed a trail from the Texas herds to the Kansas railhead town of Abilene. Cattle were already being shipped north and east by way of Sedalia, Missouri, but McCoy set in motion an industry of new dimensions. Between 1869 and 1890 perhaps as many as ten

Bill Pickett, a famous black cowboy
Courtesy Western History Collection, University of Oklahoma Library, Norman

million cattle were driven up the Texas trails to Abilene, Ellsworth, Dodge City, Wichita and Caldwell. And with this unique industry came the saga of the cowboy who drove the herds for his boss, stopped the stampedes, and held a wild celebration in the Kansas railroad towns.[12]

By the 1880s the open range cattle business had spread into Nebraska, Colorado, New Mexico and Wyoming, Montana and the Dakotas. In the Far West vast ranches developed in Oregon, California and Nevada, and for twenty years lowing herds moved across trails that could be found from the Mississippi to the Pacific. The size and extent of the operations would have captured the imagination of the dullest mind. Yet the cowboys themselves remained questionable figures, for they had the reputation of being ruffians and delinquent nomads. Indeed, "cowboy" was a term of opprobrium into the 1890s.

The image began to change slowly when John Burwell—"Texas Jack"—Omohundro, a frontier friend of Buffalo Bill's, published an article on "The Cow-Boy" in an 1877 magazine. In it, Texas Jack praised the cowboy for having the noble qualities of a hero and a poet. As Don Russell has noted, Texas Jack talked about the dangers of "bucking horses, cattle stampedes, milling cattle" and the necessity of singing to the herd at night to keep them calm.[13] Omohundro had defined the basic image for the open range cowboy that has come down to the present.

☐   ☐

To understand Cody's role in developing that image, one must look first at that unique American sport—the rodeo. On June 10, 1847, Captain Main Reid, while on visit to Santa Fe, New Mexico, described a "'round-up'... that proved to be a Donneybrook fair in which the participants contested for 'the best roping and throwing' along with 'horse races and whiskey and wine' and 'much dancing on the street.'"[14]

In the thirty years that followed, both Mexican vaqueros and Anglo-American cowboys began to participate in annual events that tested the skill and prowess of men against beasts. As early as 1872, Cheyenne, Wyoming held a "stampede" or "round-up" to celebrate the Fourth of July. Thereafter, Western towns from Prescott, Arizona to Caldwell, Kansas, began to hold rodeos as a way of reliving frontier days.[15]

Just as the open range cattle business was hitting its stride, and the rodeo was emerging as an American sport, Buffalo Bill Cody encountered show business. In 1869 Edward Z. C. Judson, a journalist who used the trade name Ned Buntline, set out west to interview Major Frank North, a frontier scout. It is said that Buntline hoped North could become a dime-novel hero; the publishing house of Beadle had begun in 1860 to exploit frontier and adventure themes in these novels with tremendous success. Whatever the facts may be, Buntline spotted Cody as someone who might be a more appropriate frontier figure. The result was an exaggerated story, entitled *Buffalo Bill, the King of Bordermen,* that appeared in New York in December 1869.

Below:
The December 23, 1869, edition of Street and Smith's *New York Weekly,* featuring the first installment of Ned Buntline's serial story, *Buffalo Bill, the King of Border Men*
Collection: Ohio State University Library, Columbus

Above:
Poster
Staff of the Wild West Show 1894
Printer: Forbes' Lithographic Co., Boston, Massachusetts
106.7 x 60.9 cm. (42 x 24 in.)
Courtesy Harold Dunn Collection in possession of Howard A. Tibbals, Oneida, Tennessee

Below:
A cattle drive
Courtesy Buffalo Bill Historical Center, Cody, Wyoming

Above:
William Levi "Buck" Taylor, "King of the Cowboys"
Courtesy Western History Collection, University of Oklahoma Library, Norman

Below:
Poster
Johnnie Baker, The Marvelous Marksman *circa* 1890
Printer: A. Hoen & Co., Baltimore, Maryland
Collection: Buffalo Bill Historical Center, Cody, Wyoming

BUFFALO BILL'S WILD WEST·
CONGRESS, ROUGH RIDERS OF THE WORLD.

JOHNNIE BAKER,
THE MARVELOUS MARKSMAN.

Buntline even persuaded Cody to appear in a Western action drama on the Chicago stage in 1872, and for the next eleven years Cody participated—acting perhaps would be too elegant a word—in dramas that consisted largely of physical feats in which Indians and villains were overcome and maidens rescued to the din of firing revolvers—loaded with blank cartridges.

The historic encounter between Cody and the cowboy finally came when Cody's success on the stage and his summer job as hunter and guide for parties touring the Plains enabled him to purchase a ranch at North Platte, Nebraska. There, in the late 1870s, he participated in "round-ups" and was impressed by the skills of his hired hands in handling horses and cattle. In 1882 he invited friends to an "Old Glory Blowout" as a way of celebrating the Fourth of July. The event was, in reality, a rodeo and a round-up, with roping contests, riding of wild horses, and other feats of skill. To Cody's surprise and pleasure, a thousand entrants appeared to compete with one another.[16]

The next year in Omaha, Cody combined the elements of his action dramas and the rodeo to produce his first Wild West show. From the very beginning, the cowboy was featured as the rider of bucking broncos and wild steers. William Levi Taylor, a tall Texas cowboy from Cody's own ranch, took the role of "Buck" Taylor, "King of the Cowboys."[17]

Others were featured as well. Johnnie Baker, a skilled marksman, was called "The Cowboy Kid." And when Annie Oakley joined the show in 1884, she was quickly considered a Westerner—though she was raised in Ohio—for she rode a horse and was a spectacular sharp shooter.[18] The cowboys rose another notch on the ladder toward heroic status when Cody had them rescue the

Facing page, top:
The Cowboy Band of the Wild West show with some of the other cast members
Courtesy Buffalo Bill Historical Cente Cody, Wyoming

Facing page, center:
A group of American cowboys agains the arena backdrop used in the Wild West show
Courtesy The Denver Public Library, Western History Department, Colorac

Facing page, bottom:
Poster
Tim McCoy's Real Wild West 1938
Printer: Tooker-Moore Lithographic C New York
104.1 x 68.6 cm. (41 x 27 in.)
Collection: Circus World Museum of Baraboo, Wisconsin

Facing page, right:
Frank Hammet, chief of American cowboys for the Wild West show
Courtesy The Denver Public Library, Western History Department, Colorad

Below:
Johnnie Baker, the "Cowboy Kid"
Courtesy The Denver Public Library, Western History Department, Colorad

Bottom:
Buffalo Bill shoots glass balls thrown b Johnnie Baker, 1901.
Courtesy The Denver Public Library, Western History Department, Colorad

Deadwood stagecoach from pursuing Indians in later shows.

The Wild West or rodeo cowboy crossed the ethnic barrier to include black rodeo stars, such as Bill Pickett, who made biting a steer's lips to make him immobile famous.[19] Mexican-American horsemen also performed in Cody's show, and later he added Argentine gauchos and Russian cossacks. Over the next five decades, generations of performers in Cody's and other Wild West shows achieved fame and glorified the cowboy image. What was so important was that anyone, of any race, could identify with the figure. It was almost inevitable that the Wild West cowboy would capture the imagination of Americans. Then, in 1887, Cody opened his show in London and the cowboy became a popular international figure as well. For the Europeans, writes Ray Allen Billington, the cowboy became the symbol of the American frontiersman.[20]

Over the next fifty years Cody's Wild West show and its scores of imitators succeeded beyond the greatest expectations. Aided by the brilliant Nate Salsbury, Cody, who was himself a poor businessman, became wealthy (though briefly), and the show became more

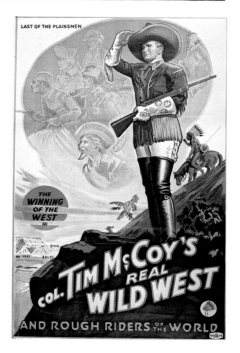

LAST OF THE PLAINSMEN

THE WINNING OF THE WEST

COL. TIM McCOY'S REAL WILD WEST

AND ROUGH RIDERS OF THE WORLD

Above:
The Wild West show cast on the beach near San Francisco, *circa* 1907
Courtesy Buffalo Bill Historical Center, Cody, Wyoming

Below:
Buffalo Bill with a group of Wild West show cowboys behind the scenes
Courtesy Buffalo Bill Historical Center, Cody, Wyoming

Facing page, left:
Chromolithograph frontispiece of the first edition of *A Texas Cowboy,* by Charles A. Siringo, published in 1885 by M. Umbdenstock & Co., Chicago

Facing page, right:
Theodore Roosevelt, rancher and cowboy, as he looked at his first round-up, 1885
Courtesy Brown Brothers, Sterling, Pennsylvania

spectacular—the dress of the performers more dramatic and ornate, thus laying the basis for the movie cowboy's costume. Cody's success was also due to the support of Colonel Prentiss Ingraham, who wrote scores of dime novels and stories about Cody and Buck Taylor as well. [21]

While Cody, Ingraham and others exploited the cowboy and his skills in shows or sensational fiction, the image and the myth were reinforced among Westerners themselves by a slight but wiry young Texan named Charles A. Siringo, who had devoured dime novels and lurid stories in the *Police Gazette* while riding the line or lounging in the bunkhouse. Convinced that he could do as well as the authors he was reading, Siringo decided to write about his own experiences. Few persons could have been better qualified, for Siringo came from Matagorda County, Texas, where as a boy he had herded cattle, skinned the hides of drowned ones, and worked on the ranch of the redoubtable Shanghai Pierce, one of the most successful ranchers in nineteenth-century Texas. Siringo participated in the long trail drives, and drank and raised hell in the cattle towns. He then drifted back to

exas and worked on a ranch near ascosa. He had also chased cattle ieves, among them Billy the Kid, to New Mexico—and on another ccasion all the way into Arizona. inally he married and settled down n Caldwell, Kansas, where he ran a gar store and ice cream parlor for ne cowboys who were herding in earby Indian Territory.

n the great American tradition of ranklin, Crockett and Cody, iringo brought out his utobiography in 1885 at the age of nly thirty. Entitled *A Texas Cowboy, or Fifteen Years on the Hurricane Deck of a Spanish Pony,* iringo's simple, cocky narrative ontained lingo and humor of the owboy, as well as stories of skill, ndurance and drunken binges. Here, in living prose, were the

pranks of an American Till Eulenspiegel.[22]

Siringo never made much from his autobiography but, hawked over the years by butcher boys on Western trains, it is supposed to have sold a million copies. *A Texas Cowboy* became, in the words of J. Frank Dobie, "the most read non-fiction book on cowboy life."[23] Siringo gave the cowboy what Cody had not: a voice and a personality that was humorous and boastful, yet attractive, gentle and romantic at the same time.

☐　　　☐

Even if Siringo had not published his life story, articulate Easterners were ready to provide a substitute. In 1884 young Theodore Roosevelt

fled west to lose himself in ranching in Dakota Territory after his wife and mother had died within a few days of one another. Within months of his arrival he boasted to a friend that "the statesman of the past has been merged into the cowboy of the present."[24] The same year that Siringo published *A Texas Cowboy,* Roosevelt published *Hunting Trips of a Ranchman* (1885). There followed other books and articles, in which Roosevelt identified masculinity and the American character with the frontier and the West. Just as Siringo had, he pursued thieves and beat up the local bully.[25] Roosevelt's Western writings, often illustrated by his friend Frederic Remington, moved the focus of the Western saga from the sensationalism of the dime novel to good writing and a respectable audience. By the turn of the century, reputable New York publishing houses and periodicals vied with one another to print Western (and often cowboy) accounts. And, less than fifteen years after his Dakota stay, Roosevelt seized the imagination of the country by organizing the "Rough Riders"—some of them Western cowboys—to fight in the Spanish-American War. The phrase "Rough Riders" appears to have

Above:
Poster
Perils of the Cowboy 1902
Printer: Courier Lithographic Co.,
Buffalo, New York
67.3 x 101.6 cm. (26½ x 40 in.)
*Collection: Buffalo Bill Historical Center,
Cody, Wyoming*

Right:
Poster
Cowboy Fun 1908
Printer: Strobridge Lithographic Co.,
Cincinnati, Ohio
76.2 x 101.6 cm. (30 x 40 in.)
*Collection: Circus World Museum of
Baraboo, Wisconsin*

een borrowed from Cody's 1893
hows, entitled "A Congress of
ough Riders." The analogy is not
o farfetched to say that just as
ody used the cowboy to rescue the
eleaguered stagecoach, Roosevelt
sed him to rescue Cuba from
upposed Spanish tyranny. In effect,
oosevelt made the cowboy, once
een as frontier bad man, an
pholder of the law and a public
ervant as well. The image was
potheosized when Roosevelt
ecame McKinley's
'ice-Presidential running mate in
900 and President in 1901. Buffalo
ill did not hesitate to include in the
Vild West show an episode
eaturing Roosevelt's Rough Riders,
nce they had become national
eroes. Some of Cody's Rough
Riders were actually veterans from
Roosevelt's troop.

Roosevelt's own success as an
magemaker, however, stemmed in
art from the paintings of Frederic
Remington, a native of New York
tate and a student at the Yale
chool of Fine Arts who went west in
881 for his health. Captivated by
he action of horse and man, the
ndian and the buffalo, and drawn to
cenes of violence, Remington
egan to produce superb sketches of
Western life, the first of which he
old in Kansas City a year after
ody's Wild West show had opened
n Omaha.[26]

By the mid-1880s Remington had
ecome famous as an illustrator, and
efore his death he had drawn
ketches for 142 books and 41
ifferent magazines dealing largely
vith the West.[27] Meanwhile, the
aintings came so fast and furiously
hat eventually he produced over
25,000. When Remington turned to
ronze sculpture, in 1895, his first
iece was a figure teeming with
owerful action and delicate grace
alled *The Bronco Buster*. With so
many exquisite works dealing with
he cowboy, Indians, horsemen and

military life in the years that
followed, Remington became as well
known for his bronzes as for his
paintings. Thus the artist not only
produced an unforgettable visual
record of the cowboy's West but
created inspiring monuments, as it
were, to a passing way of life, for by
the 1890s the open range period of
ranching had passed, and with
Western writer Badger Clark, Cody,
Roosevelt and Remington could
have chanted:

> The trail's a lane, the trail's a lane
> Dead is the branding fire.
> The prairies wild are tame and
> mild
> All close corralled with wire.[28]

Not content with painting and
sculpting, Remington also wrote
Western stories with names like
Pony Tracks (1895), *Crooked Trails*
(1898) and *Sundown Le Flare*
(1899).[29] By the turn of the century
he had come to know Theodore
Roosevelt's friend Owen Wister, an
elegant Philadelphia lawyer who had
gone west to a ranch near Buffalo,
Wyoming in 1885. Smitten with the
life of the cowboy, Wister also
vowed to capture that passing
lifestyle before it was too late. In
1902 he published *The Virginian*, a
novel about a cowboy who courted
and won the hand of a young
Eastern school marm. Dedicated to
Roosevelt, Wister's novel both

Top:
Frederic Remington
Misdeal n.d.
Oil on canvas
60.9 x 91.4 cm. (24 x 36 in.)
*Collection: Mr. and Mrs. Hal Wallis,
Los Angeles, California*

Center:
Frederic Remington
Coming Thru the Rye 1903
Bronze
Height: 69.9 cm. (27½ in.)
*Collection: Buffalo Bill Historical Center,
Cody, Wyoming*

Bottom:
Frederic Remington
Bronco Buster 1895
Bronze
Height: 56.5 cm. (22¼ in.)
*Collection: Buffalo Bill Historical Center,
Cody, Wyoming*

sentimentalized the cowboy and drew attention to the violence of his lifestyle, for the hero of the book participates in a lynching.

The Virginian is one of the most popular novels about the West ever written. James K. Folsom has called its hero the "best visualized cowboy" in fiction, a tough but gentle character who fights the villains and wins the girl. *The Virginian* also froze the Western novel at a certain stage for decades to come. By 1938 it had sold a million and a half copies, had appeared as a play, and was adapted for films and later for television.[30]

The dimensions of the cowboy image continued to expand following publication of *The Virginian*, in large part because of the appearance of another genuine cowboy on the American stage and vaudeville circuit—Will Rogers. The son of a mixed-blood family who ranched near Oolagah, Oklahoma (then still Indian Territory), Rogers proved to be extraordinarily talented at roping and riding. After serving as a cowhand in Texas and Argentina, he joined a series of Wild West shows and circuses that toured the world.[31] Rogers' brilliance in performing soon led him into vaudeville where he charmed his audience with a witty, running commentary while performing impressive rope tricks. After a stint with the Ziegfeld Follies, he went to Hollywood to star in both Western and general films. He also began to write a nationally syndicated column as well as amusing books about current events.

Will Rogers not only gave the cowboy a voice, but seemed to demonstrate that out of travel and experience could come wisdom and indeed a philosophy of life. Rogers put down pomp and pretense and glorified the ordinary man to the delight of all Americans. When he died in an aviation accident in Alaska

in 1935 at the age of fifty-six, he was mourned as a national hero.[32] Certainly Rogers came as close as anyone to personifying the qualities, experiences and accomplishments of the ideal cowboy.

Together, Cody, the dime novelists, Siringo, Roosevelt, Remington, Wister and Rogers produced a new American hero, whose image has become intertwined with the American experience today. The persistence of this image cannot be attributed to popular or sensational fiction, to the exploitation of the cowboy in art, or to the imitation of cowboy dress—whether the fad be that of jeans, hats or boots. Even the conscious adaptation of the cowboy story to the city, as has been done in the films *Midnight Cowboy* and *The Urban Cowboy*, cannot be dismissed as mere show business.

Above:
Will Rogers in *Doubling for Romeo,* a 1921 movie that poked fun at Western film cliches
Collection: The Museum of Modern A Film Stills Archive, New York

Left:
A poster for the 1946 Paramount production of *The Virginian*
Courtesy Paramount Pictures Corporation

Below:
An advertisment for Stetson hats
Collection: Buffalo Bill Historical Cen Cody, Wyoming

Below, left:
John Travolta in the 1980 Paramount production of *The Urban Cowboy*
Courtesy Paramount Pictures Corporation

Below, right:
Frederic Remington
The Rattlesnake n.d.
Bronze. Height: 55.9 cm. (22 in.)
Collection: Buffalo Bill Historical Center, Cody, Wyoming

The complexity of the cowboy image is such that it is a part of the American psyche. It stands for self-confidence, flexibility, a free lifestyle, an occupation; it symbolizes skill, represents a national sport, and serves as a subject for the serious artist, musician and writer. By both crude and sophisticated means, Buffalo Bill Cody somehow managed to sense and express the ingredients from which America's most enduring and popular myth has been formed. It is fitting that the two major centers for the preservation of cowboy culture should be the Buffalo Bill Historical Center of Cody, Wyoming, and the National Cowboy Hall of Fame in Oklahoma City, Oklahoma, a state in which so many elements of that culture first found full expression. Nor, perhaps, is it accident, given the importance of the myth in our culture, that three "cowboy-ranchers" —Roosevelt, Johnson and Reagan—have made it to the White House in this century; that is, less than a hundred years after Cody staged his Old Glory Blowout at North Platte, Nebraska in 1882. The cowboy, it seems, is in our genes.

President and Mrs. Reagan at their ranch near Santa Barbara, California
Courtesy United Press International

1. Ray Allen Billington, *Land of Savagery, Land of Promise: The European Image of the American Frontier* (New York: W. W. Norton and Company, 1981), pp. 154-58.

2. William G. "Buck" Rainey, "Guest Editors' Prologue," *Red River Valley Historical Review* 2 (Spring 1975), p. 9. This issue of the *Review* is devoted entirely to an analysis of the cowboy.

3. Joe B. Frantz and Julian Ernest Choate, Jr., *The American Cowboy: The Myth and the Reality* (Norman, OK, 1955), p. 15, quoted in Don Russell, "The Cowboy: From Black Hat to White," *Red River Valley Historical Review* 2 (Spring 1975), p. 14.

4. Russell, "The Cowboy," pp. 14-15.

5. Joe A. Stout, "Cattle Industry," in Howard R. Lamar, ed., *Reader's Encyclopedia of the American West* (New York: Thomas Y. Crowell Company, 1977), p. 174. Hereafter cited as Lamar, *Encyclopedia*.

6. Thomas D. Clark, "Davy Crockett," in Lamar, *Encyclopedia*, p. 276. See also James Atkins Shackford, ed., *David Crockett: The Man and the Legend* (Austin, TX: Pemberton Press, 1968).

7. John D. W. Guice, "Cattle Raisers of the Old Southwest: A Reinterpretation," *Western Historical Quarterly* 8 (April 1977), pp. 167-87. See also Forrest McDonald and Grady McWhinney, "The Antebellum Southern Herdsmen: A Reinterpretation," *Journal of Southern History* 41 (May 1975), pp. 147-66.

8. David Dary, *Cowboy Culture: A Saga of Five Centuries* (New York: Alfred A. Knopf, 1981), p. 72 and following. This book was consulted in page proof. See also Chris Emmett, *Shanghai Pierce, A Fair Likeness* (Norman: University of Oklahoma Press, 1953), which traces Pierce's pre-war trade with New Orleans and Cuba.

9. Russell, "The Cowboy," p. 15.

10. Cowboy clothing is discussed at length in Philip Ashton Rollins, *The Cowboy, His Characteristics, His Equipment and His Part in the Development of the West* (New York: Charles Scribner's Sons, 1922); but see also Dary, *Cowboy Culture*, pp. 14-15, 82-83; and Fay Ward, *The Cowboy at Work* (New York: Hastings House, 1958). A brief but excellent summary by Sandra L. Myres, can be found in Lamar, *Encyclopedia*, pp. 270-72.

11. The ethnic mix is well treated in Philip Durham and Everett L. Jones, *The Negro Cowboys* (New York: Dodd, Mead, 1965).

12. Joseph G. McCoy, *Historic Sketches of the Cattle Trade of the West and Southwest* (1874). Trail drivers are discussed in virtually every book on the Western frontier, but excellent coverage can be found in Ray Allen Billington, *Western Expansion: A History of the American Frontier* (New York: Macmillan, 1974), chap. 32. See also Floyd B. Streeter, *Prairie Trails & Cow Towns* (Boston: Chapman & Grimes, 1936), and Charles A. Siringo, *A Texas Cowboy* (Lincoln: University of Nebraska Press, 1966).

13. Russell, "The Cowboy," p. 17. See also Don Russell, *The Lives and Legends of Buffalo Bill* (Norman: University of Oklahoma Press, 1960), p. 305.

14.—15. Guy Logsdon, "Rodeo," in Lamar, *Encyclopedia*, p. 1028.

16. Russell, *Lives and Legends*, pp. 290—95.

17. Russell, *Lives and Legends*, pp. 298, 304—07, 389—90.

18. Walter Havighurst, *Annie Oakley of the Wild West* (New York: Macmillan, 1954), p. 20 and following.

19. Logsdon, "Rodeo," in Lamar, *Encyclopedia*, p. 1028.

20. Ray Allen Billington, *Land of Savagery, Land of Promise: The European Image of the American Frontier* (New York: W. W. Norton and Company, 1981), pp. 156—58.

21. Russell, *Lives and Legends*, pp. 273, 388—92, 496—501.

22. Till Eulenspiegel was a thirteenth- or fourteenth-century German peasant prankster whose tricks on tradespeople and jests at the upper classes were printed in a chapbook at Strasbourg in 1515.

23. Siringo's career is summarized in J. Frank Dobie's introduction to *A Texas Cowboy* (Lincoln: University of Nebraska Press, 1966), pp. ix— xxxv.

24. Quoted in George E. White, *The Eastern Establishment and the Western Experience* (New Haven: Yale University Press, 1968), p. 79.

25. See Herman Hagedorn, *Roosevelt in the Badlands* (Boston: Houghton Mifflin, 1921).

26. See Peter Hassrick, *Frederic Remington* (Fort Worth, TX: The Amon Carter Museum of Western Art, 1973); Harold McCracken, *Frederic Remington: Artist of the Old West* (Philadelphia: Lippincott, 1947).

27. Paul A. Rossi and David C. Hunt, *The Art of the Old West* (New York: Alfred A. Knopf, 1971), pp. 326—27.

28. Charles Badger Clark, Jr., "The Passing of the Trail," from *Sun and Saddle Leather* (Boston: Gorham Press, 1919), quoted in Walter Prescott Webb's *The Great Plains* (New York: Grosset and Dunlap, 1931), p. 45.

29. *Eastern Establishment*, pp. 103—07, 111—14.

30. James K. Folsom, "Owen Wister," in Lamar, *Encyclopedia*, pp. 1280—81. See also Fanny Kemble Wister, *Owen Wister Out West: His Journals and Letters* (Chicago, 1958).

31. William Richard Brown, *Imagemaker: Will Rogers and the American Dream* (Columbia: University of Missouri Press, 1970). Like so many other Westerners, Rogers wrote an *Autobiography* (1949).

32. Guy Logsdon, "Will Rogers," in Lamar, *Encyclopedia*, p. 1032.

Buffalo Bill and the Wild West

The Movies

William Judson

Curator of Film
Museum of Art, Carnegie Institute
Pittsburgh, Pennsylvania

Buffalo Bill's Wild West presented such frontier events as Custer's Last Stand, the massacre at Wounded Knee, the Battle of Summit Springs, Indians attacking a stagecoach, and Indians attacking a settler's cabin as a form of outdoor theater. These scenes were witnessed by the American public and, presumably, by fledgling Hollywood filmmakers who began making Westerns almost as soon as the medium came into being. While it is difficult to prove, it is very likely that many of Cody's arena conventions influenced the Hollywood films. For example, Cody wore a a white hat and rode a white horse, staged last minute cavalry rescues, and showed how Indians could leap onto a careening stagecoach— all stock elements of the Hollywood Western. In some of the films, Apache and Mojave braves were erroneously clothed in Plains Indian garb, either because it was what the director had seen in Cody's arena, or because Hollywood knew it was what the Cody-conditioned audiences expected to see.

In addition to affecting the idiom of Hollywood Westerns, Buffalo Bill appeared in early news-like documentary studies and produced his own historic documentaries. Since his death in 1917, more than thirty films have been produced in which he appears as a major or minor character. Nevertheless, as Bill Judson points out, his portrayals in film have not been especially accurate or perceptive. Certainly the American public's current sense of Cody, projected through the media of television and film, is vague and contradictory. [DHK]

Buffalo Bill and the movies: these would seem to be a natural combination. William F. Cody's active adult life on the frontier coincided exactly with the period of United States history that has provided material for more Hollywood movies than any other period of America's past. These years between the Civil War and the turn of the century were the years from which the Cody legends sprang, legends very much akin to those of the Hollywood Westerns. The invention of moving pictures actually occurred during Cody's lifetime. By 1895 public screenings of moving film images were attracting attention in major cities of this country and abroad, and by 1900 the moving pictures had become an important aspect of popular culture—at a time when Buffalo Bill's Wild West was also already widely known for its exciting entertainment and showmanship. In fact, Cody himself became involved in a major film project just prior to the First World War. It is ironic, then, given the extent of the convergences between Buffalo Bill and the movies, that each has been so poorly served by the other.

The Buffalo Bill mythology of the adventurous and independent frontiersman, scout and hero has never been effectively presented in film, despite more than a dozen features made after his death in which he is represented as the central character, and an equal number in which he is a secondary figure. Perhaps the very scale of the Buffalo Bill legend has contributed to the carelessness of its presentation in films; filmmakers have apparently assumed it is enough simply to include him in a picture to draw the desired response from the audience. The Buffalo Bill mythology had already taken hold in the minds of the viewing public—generated as it was by the dime novels and the Wild West show itself—and filmmakers

seem to have chosen a course of merely invoking that mythology, no establishing it or elaborating on it in any thoughtful or significant way. This has been equally true whether Buffalo Bill makes a minor appearance in a film, emblematic o his "life and times," to set the context for another story, or wheth he is himself the central character.[1]

Nevertheless, a number of the man films made over the last sixty years are of considerable interest, not simply as entertainment, but as reflections of the Buffalo Bill mythology, and of the role of film i the mythmaking process. In genera the Buffalo Bill films have evolved from a direct and uncomplicated presentation of episodes from Cody's life (with varying degrees o factual accuracy, but with a strong impresssion of actuality), to a more iconic presentation signaling the Buffalo Bill mythology. This development closely parallels a major stylistic evolution in America narrative feature films from the 1920s (the "golden age" of the silent cinema) to the 1970s.

☐   ☐

Cody's contact with film began in 1894 when he and some of his Wi West troupe, including Annie Oakley, posed for cinema portraits Thomas Edison's New Jersey Kinematograph Studio, the "Black Maria." A few years later, Cody's Wild West parade was filmed as it moved through the main streets of town somewhere in America, attracting attention for the upcomi spectacle. Film footage also exists the show's parade up Broadway in New York City. These brief glimps from an immobile camera are simi to several thousand short views fro around the world made by the tur of the century. Cameramen, particularly from France and England, traveled in Europe and North America, Asia and Africa, filming and sending home moving images from exotic lands and territorial possessions: troops in action in the Boer War, ox carts moving through the streets of Saigon and the like. The assumption was that these brief films—single takes, limited in length by the capacity of the cameras—were totally accurate depictions of real life caught on the fly. They are, indeed, documents— brief bits of recorded time, isolated like the images in a photo album for our later perusal.[2]

In the short films of Buffalo Bill and the Wild West parades, the fascination with public spectacle is clearly apparent in the indiscriminate and often unselective filming of anything that moves within the event. Equally apparent is the effectiveness of the Wild West spectacle itself in the 1890s. The camera and editing do not emphasize for us, yet we can readily discern, the impressive number of horses, and the striking contrast between the urban setting and the naturalness of riders for whom a horse serves as much more than simply main-street transportation. We even catch a fleeting glimpse of the grandness of Cody's theatrical gesture as he sweeps off his hat in salute to the obviously excited crowds. Thus these Edison films from the 1890s serve as useful records of Buffalo Bill and the Wild West.

In 1902 the Wild West was much more effectively portrayed in a film made by the American Mutoscope and Biograph Company. The arena exhibition is shown from a series of advantageously chosen viewpoints; for example, the galloping cowboys and Indians move diagonally past the camera in a path that allows the largest and clearest view of their action, while the mounted Cody himself addresses the camera's "audience" frontally, centered in the frame, acting as both the ringmaster

Buffalo Bill on parade: In an 1898 Edison film, the Wild West marches up Broadway (left, top), and Cody (in circle) doffs his hat (left, center). In a 1902 American Mutoscope and Biograph production, he plays ringmaster (left bottom), and a title (below) provides the narrative.

The World's Rough Riders introduced and led by Buffalo Bill, (Col. Wm. F. Cody)

who directs our attention and as an icon of the frontiersman, emblematic of the mythology that the Wild West already embodied. Ironically, one result of this more effective presentation in film was the replacement by the movies of many of the fairs and circuses of which the Wild West was an example.[3]

Cody himself was involved in only one major film production effort, a thorough description of which is given by the film historian Kevin Brownlow in his most recent book on the silent American cinema.[4] In 1913, Cody was engaged as the main consultant on a project to reenact major events that had occurred during the Indian Wars of the 1860s and '70s, before the invention of film. This was to be an historically accurate and ''educational'' film of Indian life, and in particular of the wars, culminating in the Battle of Wounded Knee. Unfortunately, we cannot be certain as to how these were presented, because the film, which was never permitted release by the government, allegedly decomposed at the Bureau of Indian Affairs during the 1920s.[5]

One of the events recorded was the death of Sitting Bull in 1890. Cody had not, in fact, been present when this famous Sioux chief, who had worked in the Wild West show, was shot by the Indian police. Nor had he been witness to the events at Wounded Knee, where about two hundred unarmed Sioux men, women and children were killed by the 7th Cavalry. The main technical consultant on the film project, Lieutenant General Nelson Appleton Miles, had not been present at Wounded Knee either, though as the Commanding Officer, he would presumably have been informed of what had occurred. Like Cody, Miles insisted to newspaper interviewers that he was involved in

the filming to assure that the events of Wounded Knee, and the battles of Summit Springs, War Bonnet Creek and others, were presented exactly as they happened. Both government troops and Sioux took part in the film reenactments; ironically, some of them had been involved in the original events.

Directed by Theodore Wharton, the film was sponsored in part by the *Denver Post,* which had a reporter, Ryley Cooper, on the filming location. Brownlow describes the surprising bluntness with which Cooper wrote, during the filming in 1913, of the events at Wounded Knee. Without actually using the word "massacre" to refer to that 1890 event, Cooper clearly implied it: "There the white man was the aggressor, they far outnumbering the Indians. The red men were crowded into a ravine where lines of bullets sent them to death in scores."[6] Given this unexpected openness, and the apparent insistence of Cody and Miles on historical accuracy, one can only wonder how the events at Wounded Knee and other battles were to have been presented in the film. But unless an as-yet-unknown print of it comes to light, we will be confined to speculation.

Cody's 1913 epic, *The Indian Wars:* (left, top) The capture of Sitting Bull; (center) Generals Nelson Miles, Frank Balwin and Marion Maus; (left, bottom) A crew preparing to film the scene of the Sioux being escorted to Wounded Knee; (above) Filming the military review after the battle; (below) Cody with two members of the U.S. Cavalry; (bottom) Cody leading scouts at War Bonnet Creek

Photographs left, bottom and above courtesy Buffalo Bill Memorial Museum, Golden, Colorado. All others courtesy Norman Alley Collection, California

There have survived, however, several fragments and stills from the film, in some of which we see Cody reenacting his own role in the Battle of War Bonnet Creek, and other events. What is immediately striking in these images is the characteristic theatricality of Cody's poses. Whether shading his eyes to see into the distance, or mounted like a regal statue gesturing "forward" to the cavalry troops for whom he is scouting, or crowing with pride over the captured headdress and scalp of a dead Indian adversary, Cody looks more like an actor from the Victorian stage than an actual frontier hero. Cody's experience as a performer,

The completion of the transcontinental railroad is recreated in John Ford's 1924 film *The Iron Horse.*
Collection: The Museum of Modern Art, Film Stills Archive, New York

and turn-of-the-century melodramatic notions of history, have intervened. The poses, and the pictorial compositions and camera angles, clearly convey a character playing a role—not William Cody the historical figure (however "accurately" the events may be depicted in the film), but Buffalo Bill in his mythic form: independent and adventurous, brave and victorious.

William F. Cody died in 1917, just four years after the *Indian Wars* project, at the age of seventy. The Buffalo Bill character began appearing in Hollywood movies shortly thereafter. Two of the earliest films in which he figures are *The Iron Horse* and *The Pony Express.* Both are significant films of the mid-1920s by important directors working with

historical material from the 1860s, and in each picture the character of Buffalo Bill makes a token appearance, as if only to certify the content. Both films are rooted in James Cruze's earlier picture, *Covered Wagon,* completed in 1923. Here considerable attention had been paid to the details of equipment, clothing and other authenticating elements to depict the opening of the West in the late 1820s. The box office response to this production, and the acclaim given its grand scale and historic accuracy, led directly to John Ford's *The Iron Horse* (1924) and Cruze's *The Pony Express* (1925).

The Iron Horse adopted the same large production scale as *Covered Wagon,* with a large cast and

substantial boom-town architecture. It is set later, in the 1860s, when the Republican members of Congress voted to grant public lands to the Union Pacific and the Central Pacific Railroads—with extremely favorable loan terms—to encourage the construction of a transcontinental railway. *Iron Horse* is based on the Union Pacific side of this project, in context of melodramatic fictional intrigues of love and avarice. The images of the final sequence of the film, in which the two railways are joined outside of Ogden, Utah, are directly based on photographs of the actual event in May, 1869. These well-known photographs, with the engines head to head and the crowds evenly divided left and right, were clearly posed as official

Top and above:
Scenes from James Cruze's *The Covered Wagon* (1923)
Collection: The Museum of Modern Art, Film Stills Archive, New York

Bottom, right:
Roy Stewart as Cody shooting buffalo in *Buffalo Bill on the U.P. Trail*

"documents" of the occasion, and Ford makes of them a verification of actuality by duplicating the pictorial composition in his film. Buffalo Bill's brief appearance in *Iron Horse* is also presented as verification of the historical accuracy; in a composition reminiscent of the theatrical images of Buffalo Bill himself, Ford shows Cody standing magnificently on a prairie knoll and firing his long rifle, posed like a park statue. John Ford, a prolific director for five decades, is generally known for his espousal of traditional American values and the heroic tradition. It is not surprising, then, to find that in this film he has generated a heroic image at the expense of the facts; Cody actually hunted buffalo at close range, mounted on horses specially trained for the purpose. Furthermore, while he did spend eight months in 1867—68 under contract to kill at least twelve buffalo per day to provide food for railway construction crews, this was for the confusingly named "Union Pacific, Eastern Division," in fact an entirely different railroad than the Union Pacific of the film.[7]

Iron Horse is one of the best early films to involve, however briefly, the historic presence of Buffalo Bill; *Pony Express* is another. James Cruze, after the success of his trend-setting historical reconstruction in *Covered Wagon*, devoted his next film project to that short-lived but immensely appealing moment in the opening of the West, the Pony Express. For just over a year, from April of 1860 to shortly after the first telegraphed transcontinental message in October of 1861, the speed of the Pony Express mail deliveries represented an impressive shrinkage of the effective size of the continent. For a while young Cody worked as an Express rider, making one memorable ride of three hundred and twenty-two continuous miles with stops only to eat and change horses.[8] Cody was only one rider of many, and had nothing to do with the initiation or administration of the Pony Express. However, because he later always included a Pony Express episode in his Wild West presentations, and as stories of record rides and escapes from Indians proliferated, Cody became centrally identified with the Pony Express in the public consciousness. Many Buffalo Bill films drastically exaggerate and falsify his Pony Express activities—the 1953 *Pony Express,* considered further on, is a prime example. The Cruze film of 1925, however, in keeping with the nature of the Cruze and Ford historical film projects generally, presents a more accurate picture. At the end of the film, in which we have seen the birth of the Pony Express (again in a melodramatic context of love and greed), the young boy Billy, whom we have occasionally seen throughout the film, is finally identified as Cody—and it is made clear that he will take over the mantle of premier rider on the route.

While the appearances of Cody in the Ford and Cruze films are very brief—mere token references to history—there are other films from the 1920s in which Buffalo Bill is a central figure of a script that draws heavily on the actual history of the American West. One of the more interesting of these is *Buffalo Bill on the U.P. Trail,* directed in 1925 by Frank S. Mattison with Buffalo Bill played by Roy Stewart. A number of aspects of young Cody's life are collapsed together into this film. We see him first as a Pony Express rider, galloping across the prairie in images that perfectly fit the enthusiastic descriptions of that process by Mark Twain and others at the time. In this early sequence, Buffalo Bill assists an injured Indian brave who, to today's consciousness, is painfully

stereotyped. In this brief episode, and later in the film when the Indians plot to stampede the buffalo, one can already find a fundamentally ambivalent attitude toward the Native Americans. On the one hand, they were perceived as "noble savages," respected for their integrity and freedom, admired for the purity of their relationship to nature; it is in this aspect that Cody is known as an advocate of fair treatment of the Indians. On the other hand, the Western tribes were seen as an integral part of the great American frontier, which was there to be challenged and overcome by an indomitable spirit of adventure and expansion. The government expressed this notion in the policy of "manifest destiny," which asserted an inevitable victory by a superior white race. It is in this aspect that Buffalo Bill was depicted in dime novels as the slayer of countless Indians, an aspect reinforced by continual public rehearsal of these deeds in over three decades of Wild West presentations in the United States and in Europe, and in the movies.

The melodramtic encoding of events in *Buffalo Bill on the U.P. Trail,* characteristic of the 1920s, includes the moral conflict between a parson and his runaway wife-turned-whore, and the "threat" to the community posed by a runaway slave-turned-businessman. Within such simplistic renderings of traditional values, however, there emerge factual fragments from Cody's life. After his brief introduction as a Pony Express rider, for example, Buffalo Bill is then presented as an entrepreneur engaged in land development. Indeed, in 1867, Cody and William Rose formed a partnership to establish a town named Rome on a site planned to be part of a railroad route. A railroad agent, William Webb, asked to be included in the

Facing page, top:
Moroni Olsen plays a distant and impassive Buffalo Bill (center) in the 1935 RKO production of *Annie Oakley.* Barbara Stanwyck is Annie.
Collection: International Museum of Photography at George Eastman House, Rochester, New York
Courtesy RKO Pictures, Inc.

Facing page, below:
The Stanwyck heroine engages Wild West star Toby Walker (Preston Foster) in a shooting match.
Collection: The Museum of Modern Art, Film Stills Archive, New York
Courtesy RKO Radio Pictures, Inc.

partnership, and when Cody and Rose refused, he had the railroad construction route changed and went on himself to establish Hays City.[9] This actual episode from Cody's life, presented in an engaging and casual fashion in this film, does not fit the usual notions of frontier independence reinforced in the movies.

While the Buffalo Bill films of the 1920s were generally an unblended mixture of melodrama and historical detail, there was a clear transition in the 1930s toward more classical mythic structures. *Annie Oakley,* directed by George Stevens in 1935, with Barbara Stanwyck in the title role, is a clear example. This film is a rare instance that focuses on Cody's later life, the years of Buffalo Bill's Wild West. All the main Wild West acts are here, not just the sharpshooting of Annie Oakley, but also the roping, bulldogging, bronco and steer busting, trick riding, the Indian attacks on the Deadwood stagecoach, and the cavalry attacks on the Indians. Even the costumes, the tents and settings, the Wild West signs and publicity graphics closely correspond to surviving photographs and brief films of Buffalo Bill's Wild West. This historical reconstruction, reminiscent of the films of the 1920s, also shares with those films a number of blatantly stereotyped characters and melodramatic themes. These range from the black cooks fixing the quail Annie has shot, and Annie's own family structure, to the tear-jerking relationship between Annie and Toby Walker, which depends so heavily on traditional simplifications of love and loyalty, and uses so blatantly the device in which the audience knows more than the characters.

There is a polish to this film not present in those of the 1920s, however, both in the "seamless" narrative editing and in the consistency of visual style. The lighting, the framing of shots and the extensive use of closeups mark this as a carefully controlled studio work, as opposed to the widespread use of open-air locations in the Westerns of the '20s. The emotional intensity that this hermetic visual style contributes to the Stanwyck character functions in strong contrast to the character of Cody in the film. Buffalo Bill, played by Moroni Olsen, is a distant and mostly impassive presence who provides a spiritual center to the film more by being there and looking and acting like Buffalo Bill than by any significant action. The role of Sitting Bull serves essentially the same transcendent function. Both are important figures in the narrative, presented not as characters whose acts have human motivations, but as signifiers of their respective positions: the frontier hero preserving history, and the defeated warrior living out his life in an alien culture. Whereas this aspect of Buffalo Bill in the 1920s films served as a verification of frontier history, his role—and Sitting Bull's—serve in *Annie Oakley* a more specific mythology: the *dignity* of that history in what some would describe as an "undignified" world.

The other major Buffalo Bill film of the 1930s is Cecil B. DeMille's *The Plainsman* (1937), based on F. Wilstach's novel *Wild Bill Hickok,* with Gary Cooper as a wry Hickok, Jean Arthur as the lively and whip-cracking Calamity Jane, and James Ellison as yet another uninspired Buffalo Bill. By this time, Buffalo Bill has been for the most part de-individualized—absorbed into the general iconography of the "Westerner" hero. Robert Warshow has written:

> What does the Westerner fight for? . . . The Westerner himself, when an explanation is asked of him (usually by a woman), is likely

to say that he does what he 'has to do.' If justice and order did not continually demand his protection, he would be without a calling. Indeed, we come upon him often in just that situation, as the reign of law settles over the West and he is forced to see that his day is over; those are the pictures which end with his death or with his departure for some more remote frontier. What he defends, at bottom, is the purity of his own image—in fact his honor.[10]

The Plainsman opens with Hickok encountering the just-married Cody on the steamboat dock in St. Louis. (He in fact married Louisa Frederici in 1866.) No sooner does Cody begin to set up house with his bride than he is asked to guide an arms shipment for the army through Indian country that only he knows—while Hickok has to go find out the intentions of his "old friend" Yellow Hand. As Louisa protests against these plans and the disruption of her nascent household, Hickok intones: "There are things that have to be done." And Cody: "I have to do my part."

Louisa is instantly recognizable as a characteristic figure in Western movies. Warshow describes her:

> . . . very often this woman is from the East and her failure to understand represents a clash of cultures. In the American mind, refinement, virtue, civilization, Christianity itself, are seen as feminine, and therefore women are often portrayed as possessing some kind of deeper wisdom, while the men, for all their apparent self-assurance, are fundamentally childish. But the West, lacking the graces of civilization, is the place 'where men are men'; in Western movies, men have the deeper wisdom and the women are children.

A CHRONOLOGY OF BUFFALO BILL ON FILM

Films featuring William F. Cody

Title (Production Company)		Director
1894	Seven Acts from the Wild West Show (Edison)	
1897	Buffalo Bill and Escort (Edison)	
1898	Parade of Buffalo Bill's Wild West Show (Edison)	
1902	Buffalo Bill's Wild West Parade (American Mutoscope and Biograph)	
1910	Buffalo Bill's Wild West and Pawnee Bill's Far East (Buffalo Bill and Pawnee Bill Film)	
	The Life of Buffalo Bill (Buffalo Bill and Pawnee Bill Film)	Paul Panzer
1913	The Indian Wars (Essanay and Colonel W. F. Cody Historical Pictures)	Theodore Wharton
1914	Sitting Bull—The Hostile Sioux	
	Indian Chief (American Rotograph)	
1915	Patsy of the Circus	Henry MacRae
1917	The Adventures of Buffalo Bill	

Films about Buffalo Bill

Title (Production Company)		Director	Buffalo Bill played by
1923	In the Days of Buffalo Bill (Universal Pictures serial)	Edward Laemmle	Art Acord
1924	The Iron Horse (The Fox Film Corporation)	John Ford	George Waggner
1925	The Pony Express (Famous Players-Lasky)	James Cruze	John Fox, Jr.
1926	The Last Frontier (Metropolitan Pictures Corporation of California)	George B. Seitz	Jack Hoxie
	Buffalo Bill on the U.P. Trail (Sunset Productions)	Frank S. Mattison	Roy Stewart
	Fighting with Buffalo Bill (Universal Pictures serial)	Ray Taylor	Wallace McDonald
1927	Buffalo Bill's Last Fight (Metro-Goldwyn-Mayer)	John W. Noble	Duke R. Lee
1928	Wyoming (Metro-Goldwyn-Mayer)	W. S. Van Dyke II	William Fairbanks
1930	The Indians Are Coming (Universal Pictures serial)	Henry MacRae	Tim McCoy
1931	Battling with Buffalo Bill (Universal Pictures serial)	Ray Taylor	Tom Tyler
1933	The World Changes (First National Film)	Mervyn LeRoy	Douglas Dumbrille
1935	The Miracle Worker (Mascot serial)	Armand Schaefer	Earl Dwire
	Annie Oakley (RKO Pictures)	George Stevens	Moroni Olsen
1936	Custer's Last Stand (Weiss Productions serial)	Elmer Clifton	Ted Adams
1937	The Plainsman (Paramount Pictures)	Cecil B. DeMille	James Ellison
1938	Outlaw Express (Universal Pictures)	George Waggner	Carlyle Moore
	Flaming Frontiers (Universal Pictures serial)	Ray Taylor & Alan James	John Rutherford
1940	Young Buffalo Bill (Republic Pictures)	Joseph Kane	Roy Rogers
1942	Overland Mail (Universal Pictures serial)	Ford Beebe & John Rawlins	Bob Baker
1944	Buffalo Bill (Twentieth Century Fox)	William Wellman	Joel McCrea
1947	Buffalo Bill Rides Again (Jack Schwarz Productions)	B. B. Ray	Richard Arlen
1949	Law of the Golden West (Republic Pictures)	Philip Ford	Monte Hale
1950	Annie Get Your Gun (Metro-Goldwyn-Mayer)	George Sidney	Louis Calhern
	King of the Bullwhip (Western Adventures Productions)	Ron Ormond	Tex Cooper
	Cody of the Pony Express (Columbia Pictures serial)	Spencer G. Bennet	Dickie Moore
1952	Buffalo Bill in Tomahawk Territory (Jack Schwarz Productions)	B. B. Ray	Clayton Moore
1953	Pony Express (Nat Holt Productions)	Jerry Hopper	Charlton Heston
1954	Riding with Buffalo Bill (Clover Productions serial)	Spencer G. Bennet	Marshal Reed
1958	Badman's Country (World Films)	Fred F. Sears	Malcolm Atterbury
1964	The Raiders (Revue Studios)	Herschel Daugherty	James McMullan
	Sette Ore di Fuco/Seven Hours of Gunfire	Jose Romero Marchant	Rick Van Nutter
	Buffalo Bill, L'Eroe del Far West/Buffalo Bill, Hero of the Far West	J. W. Fordson	Gordon Scott
1966	The Plainsman (Universal Pictures)	David Lowel Rich	Guy Stockwell
1974	Touche pas la femme blanche/Don't Touch the White Woman (Mara Films, Les Fims, 66 Lesser Productions, P.E.A.)	Marco Ferreri	Michel Piccoli
1976	Buffalo Bill and the Indians (Dino De Laurentis Corporation, Lions Gate Films, Talent-Associates—Norton Simon)	Robert Altman	Paul Newman

Note   The most complete chronology of Buffalo Bill on film appeared in the British Film Institute's *The Monthly Film Bulletin* 43, no. 572 (September 1976), pp. 188—89.

There are numerous situations throughout *The Plainsman* in which Cody and/or Hickok confront Louisa in this classic Western struggle, and DeMille carefully reinforces these confrontations by his blocking and framing of the shots. Western movie codes are, as well, the model for the relationship between Hickok and Calamity Jane. Warshow continues on the subject of female characters: "Those women in the Western movies who share the hero's understanding of life are prostitutes (or . . . barroom entertainers) . . . In Western movies, the important thing about a prostitute is . . . . her quasi-masculine independence . . . ."

Like Cody and Hickok, the legendary Calamity Jane has been cast in *The Plainsman* as a coded character on the Western model. There are minor variations—while she is clearly "fallen," she is not a prostitute, and her attraction to Hickok plays off against her independence—but the fundmental adherence to the model is apparent. By contrast, the Stanwyck heroine in *Annie Oakley,* acts as a woman in the context of a *masculine* world but not a Westerner world—she loses a shooting match to a male because it is expected of her, and constantly struggles against manipulative pressures to pursue a career not entirely of her own choosing. The comparison of these female leads makes clear to what extent *The Plainsman* is structured on the Western tradition described so astutely by Warshow twenty-five years ago. Hickok is presented as the archetypal Western hero, and while Cody shares those traits, he is "tainted" by civilization. Conveniently for the formula, biographical facts permit Hickok to die and Cody to survive at the end of the film.

Like *Annie Oakley, The Plainsman* is a well-crafted studio film. DeMille is

Above:
Betty Hutton plays Annie Oakley in
Annie Get Your Gun (1950)
Collection: The Museum of Modern Art,
Film Stills Archive, New York
Courtesy Metro-Goldwyn-Mayer

Right:
The real Annie Oakley (Phoebe Ann
Moses)
Courtesy The Denver Public Library,
Western History Department, Colorado

most widely known as the director of Biblical spectaculars like *The Ten Commandments*, but as early as 1915 in *The Cheat*, [11] he had demonstrated his ability to use intimate studio compositions effectively. The dramatic space that DeMille creates in *The Plainsman* ranges from the careful choreography of close-up heads moving in relationship to each other, to compressed crowd scenes, as when Calamity Jane drives back the townspeople with a whip. Even the shots of Cody, Hickok and the cavalry under Indian attack are carefully arranged studio compositions. Only in the energized low-camera shots of the Indians charging along the riverbed, and the rear-projected special effects shots of buffalo behind the spying Hickok, does the space hint at the openness of the plains. The overt studio space of the deep misty woods is apparent where Anthony Quinn, as a Cheyenne brave, recounts to Cody and Hickok, in the stock "Indian" language of the movies, the defeat of Custer—who is seen briefly in an impressively heroic apotheosis that would hardly coincide with a Cheyenne's version of events. As in the case of Stevens' *Annie Oakley*, much of the dramatic effect of DeMille's use of Western themes in *The Plainsman* derives from his orchestration of the space in which events occur.

While *The Plainsman* is actively and consciously involved with depicting Buffalo Bill and his legendary contemporaries within the thematic traditions of the Western, there wer numerous other Buffalo Bill films from the 1930s through the 1950s that were superficial "action" films. Buffalo Bill rides, and rides, and rides his faithful horse to save an endless string of imperiled maidens or incompetent Easterners in stagecoaches from savage and marauding Indians. They have as little to do with fact as they do with

Scenes from Cecil B. DeMille's *The Plainsman:* (top, left) Calamity Jane (Jean Arthur) holding off a crowd of townspeople; (top, right) Wild Bill Hickok (Gary Cooper) tending an injured Buffalo Bill (James Ellison); (center, left) Custer's Last Stand; (center, right) Indians charging along a riverbed; (bottom) A Cheyenne brave (Anthony Quinn) telling Hickok and Cody about Custer's Last Stand
Bottom photograph, collection: Section of Film and Video, Museum of Art, Carnegie Institute, Pittsburgh, Pennsylvania.
All others, collection: The Museum of Modern Art, Film Stills Archive, New York
Courtesy Paramount Pictures, Inc.

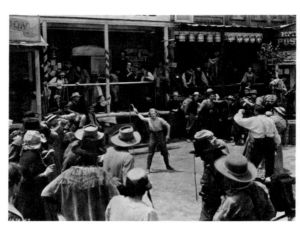

quality. In *Young Buffalo Bill* (1940), for example, a low budget Republic film with Roy Rogers as the hero and Gabby Hayes as his sidekick, Cody helps a New Mexico landowner (intended to be of aristocratic Spanish extraction) preserve his land-grant from a disloyal foreman and his Indian allies, while singing his way into the heart of the landowner's daughter. In *Buffalo Bill Rides Again* (1946), the settler and his daughter are preserved from the machinations of the evil gang and their Indian dupes by a Buffalo Bill who declares at the end, ''If I was to settle down, then I wouldn't be Buffalo Bill.'' Indeed. So he rides off on his white horse—always conveniently saddled—well-supplied with gunpowder, which he always keeps dry. A European entry in this genre is the Italian *Buffalo Bill, Hero of the Far West* (1964), which is its own ridiculous parody. The use of the name Buffalo Bill in these films has no more significance than in the game of cowboys and Indians in which one of the neighborhood kids chooses the name Buffalo Bill—or Gene Autry, Tom Mix, Red Ryder or the Lone Ranger.

Along with some of the worst Buffalo Bill films, however, there continued to appear more interesting variants. One example is William Wellman's *Buffalo Bill* (1944), in which Anthony Quinn plays a nasty Yellow Hand and Linda Darnell has the role of his stereotyped sister, an educated Indian who teaches school. The story moves from predictably trite action on the plains to an almost Felliniesque Eastern shooting gallery sequence—in which a drunken Cody rides a wooden horse—and proceeds to Washington, D.C., where, in a page from Frank Capra's naively populist *Mr. Smith Goes to Washington* (1939), Cody harangues the politicians about the rights of the Indians. This peculiar and disjointed film concludes with an

Scenes from the 1944 Twentieth Century Fox production of *Buffalo Bill:* (right, top) Linda Darnell plays an Indian teacher; (right, center) Joel McCrea is Cody on a wooden horse; (right, below) Anthony Quinn as Yellow Hand ties Cody to a stake.
Collection: The Museum of Modern Art, Film Stills Archive, New York
Courtesy Twentieth Century Fox

Left, bottom:
Poster
Buffalo Bill Rides Again 1947
55.9 x 71.0 cm. (22 x 28 in.)

emotionally loaded farewell ceremony for Buffalo Bill. This World War II picture, while again short on facts, is exceptionally effective in its hero worship.

Another interesting and equally worshipful rendition is the 1953 *Pony Express* in which Charlton Heston plays perhaps the most *macho* Buffalo Bill to have ever reached the screen, admiringly photographed from flattering angles. Says the young woman stagecoach passenger whom Cody has just saved: "I don't know how I can thank you enough." Heston replies, grinning at the camera: "I could let you kiss me." Historical facts fall by the wayside as Cody, with the help of his sidekick Hickok, is shown to be almost entirely responsible for the conception, implementation and administration of the Pony Express, which is opposed by a "maybe foreign backed" seccessionist California conspiracy.

Heston's Buffalo Bill is no longer centered on the Western hero, the thoughtful and restrained representative of justice. Instead, Heston is a swaggering adventurer (this is of course his persona in many other films as well). In *Pony Express* his pranks and friendship with Hickok anticipate the innumerable later portrayals of alienated buddies-on-the-run: *Butch Cassidy and the Sundance Kid, Pat Garrett and Billy the Kid,* television's *Alias Smith and Jones,* and so forth.[12]

Not until the 1970s did there appear films that consciously questioned the Buffalo Bill mythology. The first of these was Marco Ferreri's farcical 1974 French/Italian production of *Touche pas la femme blanche (Don't Touch the White Woman).* This film died quickly at the box office because, as Jonathan Rosenbaum reported at the time,

> . . . the notion of staging a semi-political, semi-nonsensical Western in [the markets of] Les

Above:
Joel McCrea in *Buffalo Bill*
Collection: *The Museum of Modern Ar*
Film Stills Archive, New York
Courtesy Twentieth Century Fox

Left:
Charlton Heston as Buffalo Bill in *Pony Express* (1953)
Collection: *International Museum of Photography at George Eastman Hous*
Rochester, New York
Courtesy Nat Holt Productions

Facing page:
Poster
Buffalo Bill and the Indians, or Sitting Bull's History Lesson 1974
104.2 x 68.7 cm. (41 x 27 in.)
Courtesy United Artists Corporation

Halles seems to be bewildering French audiences, even when they laugh, and neither the presence of Michel Piccoli, Marcello Mastroianni, Phillipe Noiret, and Ugo Tognazzi, nor the singular grace of Catherine Deneuve as the white woman, appears to have turned the trick . . . On the other hand, Piccoli's extravagant impersonation of Buffalo Bill—slangy American accent and swagger, Kentucky colonel countenace and all—is one of the most delightful pieces of inspired acting I've seen in a long time. [13]

More serious is Robert Altman's attempt to rethink the mythology in *Buffalo Bill and the Indians,* a film that has generated more critical response than any of the other Buffalo Bill films. Loosely based on Arthur Kopit's play *Indians,* it is certainly the most substantial of all the Buffalo Bill films, although it too has its problematic aspects. Altman's conscious intention was to call into question the *myth* of Buffalo Bill—what he stood for—and its relationship to historical facts. One of his central strategies in doing this is to call into question the film process itself at the same time. We see at the beginning, for example, an apparent Indian slaughter that is then shown by a different camera position to be a part of the Wild West performance. At other times, Paul Newman as Cody will suddenly look at or address the camera, breaking into the traditional audience role as unacknowledged voyeur. The equation here is one that a number of important filmmakers have worked with during the past two decades: traditional film *illusion* is to the unquestioned acceptance of historical myths as film *process revealed* is to an historical self-awareness and analysis. [14]

The significance of the Altman film lies in this substantial concern with the relationship between film form

Scenes from Robert Altman's *Buffalo Bill and the Indians:* (above) The Deadwood stagecoach dashes around the arena, pursued by Indians in the Wild West show; (right) Buffalo Bill (Paul Newman) talks to an interpreter (Will Sampson), while a completely disinterested Sitting Bull (Fran Kaquitts) looks away.
Collection: The Museum of Modern Art, Film Stills Archive, New York
Courtesy United Artists Corporation

and film content or meaning. In viewing it, we are constantly engaged in realizing, for example, that a composition framed by the camera *means* something quite different from what it traditonally would in film; the figure in the center of the picture may turn out not to be the most important figure, for instance. Likewise, the interplay between "real" Kodak color in some shots and "historic" sepia in others calls attention to the role—not to be taken for granted—of photographs and films as "documents." In the same way, Altman uses focus as a part of this process. The background behind Newman is often in soft focus, for instance, so that he is isolated pictorially from his surroundings in a way that engages notions of *icon*, but also so that he is the center of potentially analytic interest.

It is this concern with the intelligent use of film form and its meaning that makes *Buffalo Bill and the Indians* the most interesting of the Buffalo Bill films. Altman is obviously concerned with rectifying the grossly inaccurate popular notions of the history of the American Indians, and the role of whites in their genocide—in particular the role of mythic heroes like Buffalo Bill. But Altman's objective is impeded by an implausibly romanticized portrait of the Indians in the film. To opt, finally, for one of the two sides in the traditional historic American ambivalence toward the Indian—the "noble savage" side—contributes nothing to clarifying their history. Such a clarification needs a new

historical model, and Altman's film does not provide this. [15]

In terms of effectively reaching a large public with questions about the *process* of history, and how that process has depicted the American West, none of the Buffalo Bill films have approached, for example, Arthur Penn's *Little Big Man*, which helped to demystify the traditional cowboys and Indians model, or Altman's own *McCabe and Mrs. Miller*, which added a more human dimension to the Western action and landscape. Certainly the kind of historical revelation and analysis represented by films like Marcel Ophuls' *The Sorrow and the Pity*, which dug directly into the sacrosanct mythology of the French Resistance during World War II, has not been applied in film to Buffalo Bill.

Clearly, a large part of the strength of the myth of Buffalo Bill, shared with kindred heroes like Wild Bill Hickok and Kit Carson, comes from the fact that his is an historical character, unlike such later cowboy movie heroes as Tom Mix, William S. Hart or Roy Rogers. At the same time, Buffalo Bill and his colleagues, as plainsmen, have avoided popular association with specific events, as opposed, for example, to Wyatt Earp and the O.K. Corral. The generalized frontier mythology of Buffalo Bill is enhanced, instead, by generic actions—leading the cavalry into battle against the Indians, or protecting the stagecoach, or getting the Pony Express mail through. These kinds of actions, definitive of

the notion of the frontier hero, were of course the staple of Buffalo Bill's Wild West, together with roping, riding and marksmanship. And as the Wild West and similar shows disappeared after the turn of the century, the same generic elements were carried on in the movies.

The depiction of Buffalo Bill in the movies has evolved from the 1920s in ways that parallel the style and content of American films generally, and has naturally varied from film to film according to the acuity of the director and the substance of his script. Throughout these films, however, is the abiding notion of a traditional American hero cast in the form of the independent man of action. Teddy Roosevelt is the political figure to have most closely approximated this model, and perhaps Thomas Edison in science and industry; Buffalo Bill is as representative of this traditional hero as any American figure. This hero's achievements are generally measured by his own adherence to ideals of independence and single-handed action, and the American frontier prior to the complicating aspects of "civilization" has made an appropriate arena for him. The model has faded somewhat in recent years, as a growing awareness of the complex and interdependent social fabric make adherence to these ideals more difficult. Yet the simplicity and clarity of the struggle of man against the frontier—that last stronghold of the nineteenth century's Romantic Nature—still holds considerable appeal. No matter that William F.

Cody was involved with the horse-stealing Jayhawkers, or was a rather imperfect family man or, in fact, a real person. The mundane is easily transcended by the mythic hero, Buffalo Bill, and the human complexities of historical problems conveniently vanish in the pure light of the Great Frontiersman projected on the screens of our collective mind.

1. This assessment of the Buffalo Bill films is best considered in terms of Westerns generally, among which there have been many intelligent and well-formed productions. Accomplished narrative Westerns began as early as 1903 with Edwin S. Porter's *Great Train Robbery,* and flourished as a genre with the films of Bronco Billy Anderson, William S. Hart and others in the 'teens. By the 1920s, the Western was already a Hollywood staple. The most useful general English language history of the Westerns remains George N. Fenin and William K. Everson, *The Western: From the Silents to the Seventies* (New York: Grossman, 1973).

2. The range of early film topics is indicated by the more than three thousand titles listed in Kemp R. Niver, *Motion Pictures from the Library of Congress Paper Print Collection 1894-1912* (Berkeley and Los Angeles: University of California Press, 1967). Lists of holdings of early films in other national archives are comparable. A summary of early nonfiction film production is included in the first four chapters of Raymond Fielding, *The American Newsreel 1911-1967* (Norman: University of Oklahoma Press, 1972).

3. One of the most classic continuations of this iconic imagery in film is the last shot in the 1953 *Pony Express*, in which the admiring upward shot of the Pony Express statue has superimposed the following Lincoln quote: "A grateful people acknowledge with pride its debt to the riders of the Pony Express. Their unfailing courage, their matchless stamina knitted together the ragged edges of a rising nation. Their achievement can only be equaled—never excelled."

4. Kevin Brownlow, *The War, The West and the Wilderness* (New York: Alfred A. Knopf, 1979), pp. 224-35.

5. Brownlow, *War, West and Wilderness*, p. 228.

6. Brownlow, *War, West and Wilderness*, p. 230.

7. Don Russell, *The Lives and Legends of Buffalo Bill* (Norman: University of Oklahoma Press, 1960), pp. 88-89.

8. Russell, *Lives and Legends*, pp. 48-51. Russell, in his usual concern with separating verifiable fact from fabrication and distortion, takes care to point out that Cody's ride was not the longest Pony Express ride recorded, and that the tales of Indian encounters have been expanded or made up.

9. Russell, *Lives and Legends*, p. 84.

10. This and the following Warshow quotes are from Robert Warshow, "The Westerner," *Partisan Review*, March 1954. It has been reprinted in Daniel Talbot, ed., *Film: An Anthology* (Berkeley and Los Angeles: University of California Press, 1967) and Gerald Mast and Marshall Cohen, eds., *Film Theory and Criticism* (New York: Oxford University Press, 1974 and 1979).

11. In this impressive early film, Sessue Hayakawa plays a rich and evil character who attempts to gain financial and sexual control of a society lady played by Fanny Ward. The film was banned in some states, but had a considerable success in Paris.

12. One of the greatest differences between DeMille's 1937 *The Plainsman*, and the 1966 remake directed by David Rich, is that in DeMille's film the male protagonists are directly engaged in serious Westerner themes which the later film trivializes into jocular and counter-social horseplay. The 1953 *Pony Express* is already closer to the latter genre.

13. Jonathan Rosenbaum, "Journals," *Film Comment* 10, no. 3 (May-June, 1974), pp. 2 and 62.

14. Jean-Luc Godard is perhaps the best known and certainly one of the most seminal among a considerable number of filmmakers whose work has consistently shown this concern. There is a large body of critical and theoretical writing in this field.

15. Among the more interesting articles on this Altman film are those of Janey Place in *JumpCut*, no. 23 (October 1980), pp. 21-22; Tom Milne in *Sight and Sound,* Autumn 1976, p. 254; and Jonathan Rosenbaum in *The Monthly Film Bulletin* 43, no. 512 (September, 1976), pp. 188-89.

Buffalo Bill and the Wild West

The Legend

Leslie A. Fiedler

Samuel Clemens Professor of English State University of New York, Buffalo

Buffalo Bill was America's first media hero. He became famous in dime novels, was a well-known figure on the stage, became the subject of well-crafted publicity and promotion, and starred as the highly visible master of ceremonies in his own extravaganzas.

In writing about Cody's many manifestations, Leslie Fiedler focuses on Buffalo Bill as a show business phenomenon created by hack writers and nurtured by press agents. He sees Cody's persona as comprising a complex of legends which satisfied certain psychological needs and mythic expectations of his public but rendered the real man indistinguishable from his image.

Even today, Fiedler contends, the Buffalo Bill legend defies satisfactory interpretation by analysts determined to unmask the reality. As he shares his impressions of Buffalo Bill-as-fiction, he identifies for us the archetypes of the enduring Western myth. Was William F. Cody an authentic Western hero? Fiedler asks if it is necessary, or even desirable, to seek a "truth" or reality behind the legend. [DHK]

Above:
Poster
Portrait *circa* 1900
Printer: Enquirer Job Printing Co., Cincinnati, Ohio
3-sheet: 204.5 cm. x 106.7 (80½ x 42 in.)
Collection: Circus World Museum of Baraboo, Wisconsin

Right:
Louisa Frederici Cody, Buffalo Bill's wife *circa* 1860
Courtesy Buffalo Bill Historical Center, Cody, Wyoming

For more than a century now the image of Buffalo Bill has captured the deep imagination of Americans. Most of us still see in our mind's eye that erect figure astride a white horse, ten-gallon hat in hand or pushed back just a little to reveal the ruddy complexion, the startlingly brown eyes, the silky mustache and goatee—becoming, like his almost shoulder-length hair, whiter and whiter with the passage of the years. "Buffalo Bill," we say to ourselves, and the magical name evokes the legend that, though it may these days trouble rather than inspire us, refuses to die. Not only has it outlasted the Old West that was its setting, the Indian wars that were its immediate occasion, and even William F. Cody, the actual man whose not very extraordinary life it transformed into a unique American dream; it has survived as well the vogue of the illustrated pulp fiction and the popular drama in which it was first embodied.

The Western frontier was already closing by the 1880s, and the last large-scale slaughter of Indian "hostiles" by white troops began with the shooting of Sitting Bull in 1890 and culminated two weeks later with the massacre at Wounded Knee. Cody himself was not present at either event, the first of which he had in fact futilely attempted to prevent—thus losing his chance of dying in an Indian ambush or shootout, as the myth that he had lived seemed for a while to demand. To be sure, there was a war in progress in 1917 when he finally died, and America was becoming involved in it; but it was a European conflict removed from his myths of westward expansion and heroism in the "Great Desert" of the Plains. In any case, Cody had by then become embroiled in the anti-mythic world of business and domesticity, fighting his last battle not at Ypres or Verdun

but in a Wyoming courtroom, where he sued for divorce his embittered wife, convinced she was trying to poison him. It was she who emerged the victor, however—or at least had the last laugh—since the divorce was not granted, and she was therefore able, despite Cody's expressed wish, to have him buried far from the Wyoming city that bears his name but does not even now possess his remains.

His spirit, however, lived on after his death for nearly two decades in the Wild West, the open-air historical pageant and equestrian display that he had first mounted in 1883, and in which he starred until 1916, when he could no longer sit in a saddle but entered the arena holding the reins of a horse-drawn carriage—a tremulous old man, bewigged and grease-painted into an unconvincing simulacrum of his former self. None of this mattered, however, anymore than it mattered that the ownership of his show had long since passed into the hands of Pawnee Bill—who combined it with his own "Far East"—and the Sells-Floto Circus, which combined the remnants of

Top, center:
The last known photograph of Col. and Mrs. Cody, taken at a train depot, 1912
Courtesy Buffalo Bill Historical Center, Cody, Wyoming

Top, right
Poster
Still Holds the Reins n.d.
Printer: Russell & Morgan Printing Co., Cincinnati, Ohio
71.1 x 104.1 cm. (28 x 41 in.)
Courtesy Harold Dunn Collection in possession of Howard A. Tibbals, Oneida, Tennessee

Above:
Buffalo Bill in 1915
Courtesy The Denver Public Library, Western History Department, Colorado

Left:
Poster
Iron Tail *circa* 1900
Printer: Enquirer Job Printing Co., Cincinnati, Ohio
76.2 x 50.8 cm. (28 x 20 in.)
Collection: Circus World Museum of Baraboo, Wisconsin

Left, below
Poster
Buffalo Bill's Wild West and Sells-Floto Circus *circa* 1914
Printer: Erie Lithographic and Printing Co., Erie, Pennsylvania
Collection: Buffalo Bill Historical Center, Cody, Wyoming

Above:
A cartoon from the *Boston Evening Record* of January 15, 1917
Courtesy Buffalo Bill Historical Center, Cody, Wyoming

Bottom:
A dinner in honor of Buffalo Bill (inside square) given by the Showman's League of America at Chicago's Hotel La Salle, March 15, 1913
Courtesy Buffalo Bill Historical Center, Cody, Wyoming

Buffalo Bill's original cast of Indians, cowboys, trick riders and sharpshooters with freaks, sword-swallowers and tattooed ladies. All that those last audiences required was Buffalo Bill's physical presence, his hand lifted in a valedictory gesture that countless repetitions did not stale, turning it rather into a ritual reassurance that a vanishing America and the breed of American who made it had not *quite* vanished from the earth. Not yet.

Even his actual demise seems to have made little difference in this respect; for though it moved old rivals to posthumous judgments (Pawnee Bill observing "He was just an irresponsible boy") and new poets to elegiac verses (E.E. Cummings writing, "Buffalo Bill's/defunct . . . Jesus/he was a handsome man . . ."), the Wild West continued on, as if he had never died at all. Symptomatically, however, the last two such shows, both of which closed in 1938, were produced by a pair of film cowboys, Tim Holt and Tom Mix, whose quite different icons and myths the oldsters among us remember as projected in the darkened theater rather than acted on a dusty field under the open sky.

But almost no one living any longer recalls the illustrated dime novels or the stage melodramas in which the image and legend of Buffalo Bill were first created. In fact, well before 1938—when the Great Depression was about to end and World War II about to begin—Ned Buntline, who wrote the first of those novels and the second of those plays, was nearly forgotten; and Prentiss Ingraham, who produced more Buffalo Bill fiction than any other author, was fast fading into oblivion.

Even novels signed if not actually authored by Cody himself were already gathering dust in attics and on the shelves of children's libraries, along with the various versions of his *Autobiography* and his sister's account of his life—once sold on street corners for a dollar (a ticket of admission thrown in free) by the advance men for his show. As they died from memory, so too did the black-and-white steel engravings, "The First Scalp for Custer," "Bloody Work of the Squaws," "A Hurricane of Buffalos," with which they were adorned, as well as the full-color reproductions of the same motifs on the hundred-sheet billboard posters, and the autographed photos of Cody and his fellow performers. The pictures had gone into oblivion along with the words.

Or if not quite into oblivion, into the hands of PR men eager to attract tourists to one or another of the competing Buffalo Bill Centers in Colorado and Wyoming, or scholars dedicated to discovering the "historical truth" behind the icons and myths. To be sure, Cody had always claimed that it was just such "truth" ("Everything Genuine!") that was enacted in his Wild West, which he would therefore never allow anyone to call a "show." Yet from childhood on, the evidence seems to indicate, he had longed to become a showman, telling his sisters in intervals between "playing Indians" (he, the sole surviving male member of his family, was always the scalper—they invariably the scalped) that "I believe I'll run a show when I get to be a man." And when they objected that this ill befitted one destined—as a fortune teller had revealed to their mother—to be President of the

United States, he answered, "I don't propose to be President, but I do mean to have a show."

He ended, moreover, as he had begun, playing "Cowboys and Indians"—at first, just behind the elusive frontier at North Platte, Nebraska, where in 1882 he celebrated the Fourth of July with an "Old Glory Blowout," then in the parks and fair-grounds of urban centers like Chicago, Boston and New York, Paris, London and Rome. But for ten years before 1882 he had impersonated in the indoor theaters of countless cities and towns a mythological hero called by his name, who night after night killed Indians and delivered female captives from a fate worse than death. It was a plot first naturalized in America by James Fenimore Cooper, then readapted to the prairie West by Ned Buntline, Prentiss Ingraham and other best-selling novelists in quest of a new theme. But on the stage, they discovered, such stories had an added appeal when enacted by *real* frontiersmen and scouts, like Cody himself or Texas Jack Omohundro and Wild Bill Hickok, who joined him in some of his first dramatic ventures.

It scarcely mattered if these men forgot their lines or broke character, since the audiences came in large part to see them not *in* but *through* parts they played, returning, once the season was over, to their part-time roles as real killers of beasts and men. Buffalo Bill, in particular, as all readers of newspapers and magazines were kept aware, had never abandoned the wilderness life that had first made him famous. When the theaters

closed for the summer of 1872, for instance, he went back to his old haunts as guide to a buffalo-hunting party that included the Grand Duke Alexis of Russia. And four years later, between theatrical seasons, he rejoined the 5th Cavalry, just in time to avenge Custer by scalping an Indian called Yellow Hand. That redoubtable deed he apparently performed dressed in a particularly splendid costume he had first worn on the stage, and in the presence of an audience of newspapermen. Furthermore, no sooner had he gotten back to "civilization," than he appeared in a new play called *The Red Right Hand; or Buffalo Bill's First Scalp for Custer*—as if fact and fiction were not merely continuous but indistinguishable.

The confusion between reality and illusion, history and myth was even further confounded by the fact that with the opening of the Wild West show, no one wrote a fictional script; and the reenactments of fact directed by Buffalo Bill himself employed not professional actors but real cowboys, real Indians, real cattle and horses and mules and bison. Consequently, when Custer's Last Stand was reenacted in the arena, half of the cast—all Indians, of course—had participated in the original battle.

Finally, even the most infamous "hostile" of all, Sitting Bull, joined the show for one season, and when he left, he took with him two presents from Buffalo Bill: a size eight white Stetson and a dancing horse he particularly admired. Indeed, even as he was gunned down in a tragicomedy of errors by a fellow tribesman who was trying to prevent his arrest, that horse, taking

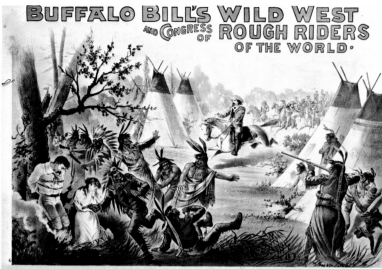

BUFFALO BILL TO THE RESCUE.

Left:
Poster
To the Rescue *circa* 1894
Printer: A. Hoen & Co., Baltimore,
Maryland
71.1 x 97.8 cm. (28 x 38½ in.)
*Collection: Buffalo Bill Historical Center,
Cody, Wyoming*

Below:
Poster
**Chief of Scouts and Guide for U.S.
Army** *circa* 1875
Printer: A. Hoen & Co., Baltimore,
Maryland
64.8 x 50.8 cm. (25½ x 20 in.)
*Collection: Buffalo Bill Historical Center,
Cody, Wyoming*

the shot for his customary cue, w
into his customary dance. And wl
was to say that he was wrong, tha
what happened was not, in some
sense, a part of Buffalo Bill's
ongoing mythological show.

☐   ☐

Fair enough, then, that when in tl
troubled 1960s the history of the
American West was being rewritte
Buffalo Bill, flanked by Sitting Bu
reappeared in the theater not as
"The Last of the Great Scouts," t
as a showman playing a part. In
Arthur Kopit's *Indians,* a play
produced in New York in 1969,
Cody enters bowing to an unseer
audience from the back of a
palpably fake white stallion. He is
ghost called back not to the real
world but to an equally ghostly
stage—or rather a spectral "Wild
West," which, like him, cannot q
die. It is metatheater with which v
are confronted, theater about
theater; though the play within a
play, once so vast it could scarcely
be contained in acres of open fiel
can now be enclosed by a
proscenium arch. Buffalo Bill has
likewise been reduced in scale, al
with Wild Bill Hickok and Ned
Buntline, and indeed everyone
involved—except for the Indians,
who are larger than life, larger tha
death, and for whom the play is
therefore named.

Nor is this inappropriate to a time
when revisionist anthropologists
were glorifying the Indian way of
and revisionist historians recastin
them as the "good guys" rather tl
the "bad" in the struggle for the
Western Plains. There were also
revisionist novels and films,
which—in response to growing
feelings of white guilt and self-hat
vis à vis the native people of
America—travestied and traduce
all myths justifying Westward
expansion. Sentimentalization of
"Noble Savage" had had a place

Top, Left:
Stacy Keach, Jr., as Buffalo Bill in Arthur
Kopit's *Indians*, New York, 1969
Photograph: Martha Swope, New York

Top, right:
Painted glass advertisement for
Chancellor cigars, *circa* 1900
*Collection: Buffalo Bill Historical Center,
Cody, Wyoming*

Left:
Alick P. F. Richie
Untitled 1903
Illustration for poster
Oil on board
75.9 x 49.2 cm. (29⅞ x 19⅜ in.)
*Collection: Buffalo Bill Historical Center,
Cody, Wyoming*

our literature from the start, but it
had typically been balanced by
vilification of his "innate barbarism."
In the late '60s, however, the latter
was neutralized and the former
reinforced by the mounting protest,
occasioned by our involvement in
Vietnam, against not merely all war
and racism, but against the very
concepts of patriotism and combat
heroism—except as practiced by
warriors of another color.

The favorite reading matter of the
period, especially among the young,
included Claude Lévi-Strauss'
Pensée Sauvage, John G. Neihardt's
Black Elk Speaks, Theodora
Kroeber's *Ishi in the Two Worlds,*
Dee Brown's *Bury My Heart at
Wounded Knee,* Vine Deloria, Jr.'s
Custer Died for Your Sins, Ken
Kesey's *One Flew Over the
Cuckoo's Nest* and Thomas Berger's
Little Big Man—all of them defenses
of Indian culture and attacks on the
whites who sought to destroy it,
some directed specifically at George
Armstrong Custer. Once Custer had
been thus "debunked," however,
Buffalo Bill's legend was doomed,
since he was in some sense the
General's *alter ego*. The Plains

Right:
The Wild West show's attack on the
Deadwood stagecoach
*Courtesy The Denver Public Library,
Western History Department, Colorado*

Above:
"Buffalo Bill Saves a Lady from the
Indians," the Deadwood stagecoach act
at Madison Square Garden
Courtesy The Bettmann Archive, Inc.

Indians called both by the same name, Pahaska, or Longhair, and in fact they bore an uncanny resemblance to one another—which Cody seems deliberately to have exploited, modeling his persona on that of the professional soldier who had gone down to defeat before the Wild West show began. So faithful was his impersonation that seeing him in the arena years later, an old black maid of the Custers was stunned to discover in him the express image of her former master. But he had the right, Cody would have protested, since he had not only served under Custer but had "avenged" him with the scalping of Yellow Hand.

Moreover, not just their icons but their myths were the same, the archetypal meanings of the Wild West and the Battle of the Little Big Horn being finally one. We are used, however, to looking for myth in story; and at first glance, Cody's "exhibitions" seem to have had no more narrative line than a three-ring circus. Yet once we have understood that the sharpshooting, the rodeo events and the general highjinks are secondary—a concession to the audience demand for entertainment and vicarious tourism—we can locate in the Wild West, if not a continuous story, at least a mythic center, represented by such

standard features as the attacks on the Deadwood stagecoach, the immigrant train or the settler's cabin; the duels with Tall Bull or Yellow Hand; and Custer's Last Stand itself.

Reflecting on these, it becomes clear that the theme of Buffalo Bill's Wild West was more specifically guerrilla warfare, in which individual combat skills still counted—as they had not in the Civil War, whose outcome was decided by technology rather than personal heroism. By the time Cody's theatrical career began, the dreadnought and the machine gun had already been invented, and before his last appearance in the arena, the armored car, the tank, the zeppelin and the combat plane were already in action. Nonetheless, the forces of good in the Wild West continued right to the end to fight on horseback and with Colts and Winchesters against a similarly mounted and armed enemy, who possessed such weapons and mounts in the first place because they had been given or sold them by the whites.

What motivated them to do so is hard to say—blind greed, perhaps, or some dim sense of fair play, or even an unconscious desire to make possible the last war white America could unequivocally win, and the reassuring mythic drama into which Buffalo Bill converted it. In any event, it is almost impossible to tell where the real Wild West ends and the Wild West show begins, since

they have the same cast: Indians and cowboys, horses and soldiers. Of these, it is the Indians and horses whose names we remember (Long Bull and Sitting Bull, Brigham, Powderface and Charlie), while their white opponents fade to an anonymous blur—except, of course, for Buffalo Bill himself. Cody's Indians, moreover, moved, like him and his horses, back and forth between history and show biz, which is to say, warring and playing at war. Indeed, one of the strangest aspects of the spectacle he created was that in it the defeat of the "Redskin hostiles" was acted out by the defeated themselves—repeating endlessly, as if in a recurrent nightmare, the events that had turned them from fighters against the white man's culture to actors in a white man's show.

Most of the Indians were, it is true, wards of the government; many actual Prisoners of War, like the survivors of the Ghost Dance, nineteen of whom were released in Cody's custody for one of his grand European tours. But why they consented to reenact their humiliation before an audience of their conquerors I find puzzling, though—even more oddly—earlier commentators on the Wild West seem not at all troubled by so unprecedented an event. To be sure, conditions were bad back on the reservation, and the Indians were paid well by Cody, fed well, provided with cigarettes and

...ansported to foreign lands where they were paid a great deal of attention and admired. The world of illusion, moreover, was one in which they felt at home. Indeed, one recent anthropologist has called the whole culture of the Plains Indians "as make-believe as the set of a Western movie." Even in war, they seemed motivated more by a desire to win the applause of their peers than to destroy their enemies; so that ritually touching the body of a foe in combat was deemed as authentic a *"coup"* as stabbing him in the heart. But in this case, it was on their living bodies that *coups* were counted over and over, and to endure this, they must in some sense have subscribed to the myth as well as to the fact of their defeat.

Indeed, it is reported that Short Bull, one of the organizers of the Ghost Dance (that last piece of "make believe" in which the Sioux came to believe they would be delivered from the white man), said of Cody, "He killed us because we were bad and because we fought against what he knew was best for us. . . ." But what "he knew was best" was, of course, that "the inferior must give way to the superior civilization . . . Their doom is sealed . . . The total extinction of the race is only a question of time." These words were written by Cody's sister, who framed them with a reference to Cooper's *Last of the Mohicans*—in which the Myth of the Vanishing American was first formulated—and a quotation from Kipling's "The White Man's Burden." Elsewhere, moreover, Cody himself further specifies what his sister means by "white," insisting that the West can only be redeemed from "Savagery" by "the march of the Anglo-Saxon race," at whose head his more ardent fans liked to imagine him, a White Knight on a White Horse.

If the chivalric metaphor out of Sir Walter Scott reminds us

Right:
A page from an 1899 edition of *The Rough Rider*
Courtesy The Denver Public Library, Western History Department, Colorado

Left:
Sioux prisoners at Fort Sheridan, Illinois, 1891, who later went to Europe with Buffalo Bill's Wild West. Back row standing, from left: Revenge, Take the Shield Away, Bring White Horse, Know His Voice, One Star, Kills Close to Lodge, Hard to Hit, One Bull or Lone Bull, Standing Bear, Scatter, Sorrel Horse, Horn Eagle; front row; Crow Cane or White Beaver, Medicine Horse or Plenty Wound, Call Her Name or Run By, Kicking Bear and Short Bull.
Courtesy Fort Sheridan Museum, Illinois

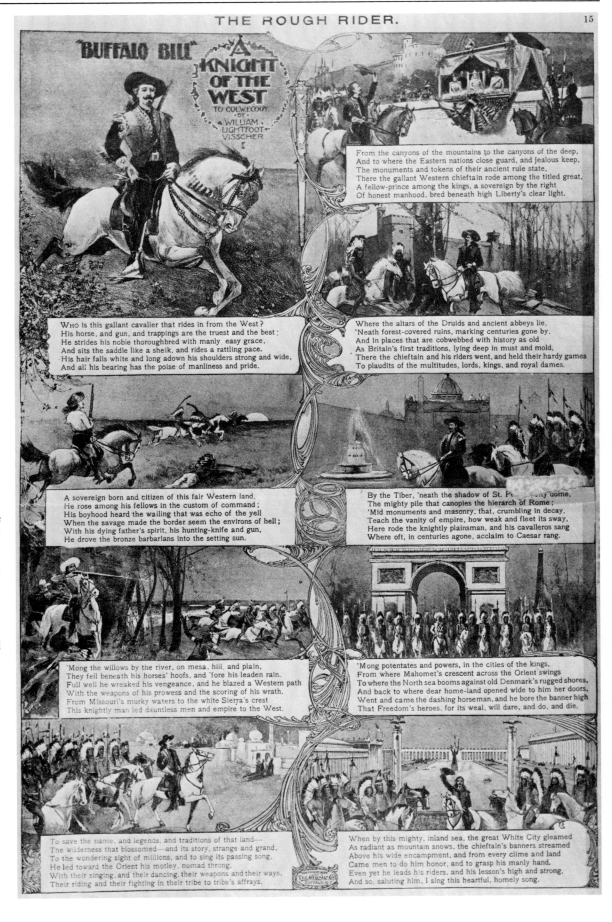

Facing page:
Poster
The Death of Chief Tall Bull 1907
Printer: Courier Lithographic Co.,
Buffalo, New York
12-sheet: 264.2 x 302.0 cm. (104 x
118½ in.)
Collection: Buffalo Bill Historical Center,
Cody, Wyoming

Above:
Scenes from Robert Altman's *Buffalo Bill
and the Indians:* Paul Newman as Cody
tells lunch guests (top) how he killed an
Indian chief, and tries to talk to Annie
Oakley (center), played by Geraldine
Chaplin.
Collection: The Museum of Modern Art,
Film Stills Archive, New York
Courtesy United Artists Corporation

uncomfortably of the sheeted riders of the Ku Klux Klan, it is fair enough, since Ned Buntline, who first launched Cody's legend, was also a leader of the American Protestant Association, that other, earlier sodality dedicated to preserving the purity of White Protestant America. And there seems to me little doubt that to many in his audiences Bill Cody represented the savior of the WASPs (the line of descent from him to John Wayne is unbroken) who, even as they were exterminating the dusky enemy in the West, were being threatened from the opposite direction by immigrant hordes out of Eastern and Southern Europe, almost equally dusky and dangerous.

Different as he was from such new Americans, however, the mythic Buffalo Bill, self-made, self-educated and of humble origins, was equally unlike certain rich and privileged older Americans, who though kin to him ethnically, had grown fat and flabby in the effete East. To them he seemed a kind of Noble Savage, a White Indian, doomed like the Red Ones to "vanish" before the advance of the civilization for which he had cleared the way, but in which he could not survive. This, at any rate, is the way in which he and his cohorts were perceived by such representatives of that world as Frederic Remington, an aging athlete from Yale, full of self-hatred and ambivalent love for the "human brutes" of the West, to which he returned again and again as a tourist and illustrator. "As a picture, perfect; as a reality, horrible," Remington wrote—and it is difficult to tell whether he is talking about cowboys or Indians—yet he was a faithful fan of the Wild West.

When the legend of Buffalo Bill passed into the hands of the descendants of East European immigrants, however—new Americans mythologically not quite

"white" and politically rather to the Left—they found him not "poetical and harmless" (as Remington had also said of the show) but racist and reactionary. They were, therefore, not inclined to mourn, even condescendingly, the passing of his kind—aware that, in fact, his heirs still survived as unreconstructed "rednecks," ready to resist with force the renewal of Indian nationalism at Alcatraz or Wounded Knee.

There is a kind of vestigial, qualified sympathy for Cody in Kopit's *Indians,* a sense that to be trapped as he was in an outlived myth, even of his own making, was at least pitiful, if not downright tragic. However, in the film "suggested" by that play but drastically rewritten by Robert Altman and Allan Rudolph, Buffalo Bill fares much worse, which is particularly ironic in light of the fact that his icon and myth had until then proved unamenable to screen treatment. In Altman's film, *Buffalo Bill and the Indians, or Sitting Bull's History Lesson,* Cody is portrayed as a bluster and bluff, a hopeless drunk, an aging swinger on the verge of impotence—and especially as an exploiter of Indians whom he neither loves nor understands.

It is Altman's Sitting Bull, magician and prophet, who understands everything, and chiefly that Buffalo Bill is the enemy and his myth of the West, a "lie" But among the whites no one heeds his "lesson" except for Annie Oakley, who is portrayed sympathetically—in accord with the liberal clichés of the time (it was 1976 before the film appeared), which demanded that women like Indians be shown as wiser than white males. Between them, in any case, they baffle, defeat and finally abandon not just Cody but his myth.

The anti-myth that Altman and Rudolph seek to substitute for Cody's proves also to be a "lie," though one more responsive to the

Buffalo Bill in 1905
*Courtesy Buffalo Bill Historical Center,
Cody, Wyoming*

psycho-social needs of the time.
What documents survive indicate
that Sitting Bull and Annie Oakley
really loved and trusted Buffalo Bill
to the end of their lives, the former
saying to a relative who dared lay
hands on his white Stetson, ''My
friend Longhair gave me this hat. I
value it very highly for the hand that
placed it on my head had friendly
feeling for me,'' while the latter
wrote of Cody, ''I travelled with him
for seventeen years . . . And the
whole time we were one great family
loyal to a man . . . His words were
more than most contracts. . . .''

But such discrepancies are finally
irrelevant, since no age can tell—or
indeed, know—the ''truth'' about the
past, but can only replace old myths
with new ones, for a little while
believing them to be ''facts.'' So with
the myth of the Winning of the West
and the subjugation of the Plains
Indians. Yet no matter how much
that myth has changed in response
to our changing attitudes over the
past century or more, the icon of the
''The Last of the Great Scouts'' has
remained unchanged at its center:
an aging horseman charging toward
us as if forever in a cloud of dust, his
hat in one hand, the reins in the
other, long white hair streaming out
behind him. And who can doubt that
as long as America lasts and memory
endures, somewhere at the heart of
the next myth we take for truth will
be the dream figure of Buffalo Bill.
''Jesus/he was a handsome man . . .''

Above:
Col. and Mrs. Cody with grandchildren
and friends at the Irma Hotel, Cody,
Wyoming, 1915
*Courtesy Buffalo Bill Historical Center,
Cody, Wyoming*

Left:
Buffalo Bill and children
Courtesy Don Russell, Elmhurst, Illinois

Bibliography

Clemens, Samuel L. [Mark Twain]. "A Horse's Tale," *Harper's Monthly*, CXIII (August-September, 1906), 328-342, 539-549.

Cody, Louisa Frederici, and Courtney Ryley Cooper. *Memories of Buffalo Bill.* New York and London: D. Appleton & Co., 1919.

Cody, William Frederick, *An Autobiography of Buffalo Bill.* New York: Cosmopolitan Book Corp., 1920.

Cooper, Courtney Ryley. *Annie Oakley, Woman at Arms.* Duffield & Co., 1927.

DeWolff, J.H. *Pawnee Bill (Major Gordon W. Lillie) His Experience and Adventure on the Western Plains.* Pawnee Bill's Historic Wild West Company, 1902.

Fowler, Gene. *A Solo in Tom-Toms.* New York: Viking Press, 1946.

Havighurst, Walter. *Buffalo Bill's Great Wild West Show.* New York: Random House, 1957.

Kopit, Arthur. *Indians.* New York: Hill & Wang, 1969.

Leithead, J. Edward. "Buffalo Bill Novels in Paperback Book Format," *Dime Novel Roundup*, XVII (June, 1949), 49-53.

Monaghan, Jay. *The Great Rascal.* Boston: Little, Brown and Company, 1952.

Murray, Marian. *Circus: From Rome to Ringling.* New York: Appleton-Century-Crofts, 1956.

Neihardt, John G. *Black Elk Speaks.* New York: William Morrow & Co., 1932.

Remington, Frederic, illustrator. "Behind the 'Wild West' Scenes," text by Julian Ralph. *Harper's Weekly*, XXXVIII (August 18, 1894), 775-776.

Russell, Don. *The Lives and Legends of Buffalo Bill.* Norman: University of Oklahoma Press, 1960.

Salsbury, Nate. "The Origin of the Wild West Show," "Wild West at Windsor," "At the Vatican," *Colorado*, XXXII (July, 1955), 204-215.

Sell, Henry Blackman, and Victor Weybright. *Buffalo Bill and the Wild West.* New York: Oxford University Press, 1955.

Smith, Henry Nash. *Virgin Land.* Cambridge: Harvard University Press, 1950.

Vestal, Stanley [Walter S. Campbell]. *Sitting Bull, Champion of the Sioux.* Boston: Houghton Mifflin, 1932; Norman: University of Oklahoma Press, 1957.

Wetmore, Helen Cody. *Last of the Great Scouts.* Chicago and Duluth: Duluth Press Publishing Co., 1899.

Buffalo Bill and the Wild West

Selected Bibliography

Andrist, Ralph K. *The Long Death,* New York: Macmillan, 1964.

Arnold, Elliott. *Blood Brother,* ed. Dale Nichols. New York: Hawthorn Books, 1947.

Billington, Ray Allen. *America's Frontier Heritage.* New York: Holt, Rinehart & Winston, 1966.

_____. *Frederic Jackson Turner: Historian, Scholar, Teacher.* New York: Oxford University Press, 1973

_____. *Land of Savage, Land of Promise: The European Image of the American Frontier.* New York: W. W. Norton and Company, 1981.

_____. *Western Expansion: A History of the American Frontier.* New York: Macmillan, 1974.

Bleiler, E. (ed.). *Eight Dime Novels.* New York: Dover Publications, 1968.

Born, Wolfgang. *American Landscape Painting: An Interpretation.* Westport, CT: Greenwood, 1948.

Brown, Dee. *Bury My Heart at Wounded Knee.* New York: Holt, Rinehart & Winston, 1971.

Brown, William Richard. *Imagemaker: Will Rogers and the American Dream.* Columbia: University of Missouri Press, 1970.

Brownlow, Kevin. *The War, the West and the Wilderness.* New York: Alfred A. Knopf, 1979.

Catlin, George. *Adventures of the Ojibeway and Ioway Indians in England, France and Belgium.* 2 vols. London: 1852.

_____. *Catalogue of Catlin's Indian Gallery of Portraits, Landscapes, Manners and Customs, Costumes, &c, &c.* New York: Piercy & Reed, 1837.

_____. *Letter and Notes on the North American Indians,* ed. Michael M. Mooney. New York: C. N. Potter, 1975.

Cody, Louisa Frederici, and Courtney Ryley Cooper. *Memories of Buffalo Bill.* New York and London: D. Appleton & Co., 1919.

Cody, William Frederick. *An Autobiography of Buffalo Bill.* New York: Cosmopolitan Book Corp., 1920.

Cooper, Courtney Ryley. *Annie Oakley, Woman at Arms.* New York: Duffield & Co., 1927.

Dary, David. *Cowboy Culture: A Saga of Five Centuries.* New York: Alfred A. Knopf, 1981.

Deloria, Vine, Jr. *Custer Died for Your Sins: An Indian Manifesto.* New York: Macmillan, 1969.

De Tocqueville, Alexis. *Democracy in America.* New York: Doubleday Anchor Books, 1969.

DeWolff, J. H. *Pawnee Bill (Major Gordon W. Lillie) His Experience and Adventure on the Western Plains.* Pawnee Bill's Historic Wild West Company, 1902.

Durham, Philip, and Everett L. Jones. *The Negro Cowboys.* New York: Dodd, Mead, 1965.

Emmett, Chris. *Shanghai Pierce, A Fair Likeness.* Norman: University of Oklahoma Press, 1953.

Fenin, George N., and William K. Everson. *The Western: From the Silents to the Seventies.* New York: Grossman, 1973.

Field, Matthew C. *Prairie and Mountain Sketches.* Norman: University of Oklahoma Press, 1957.

Fielding, Raymond. *The American Newsreel 1911—1967.* Norman: University of Oklahoma Press, 1972.

Fowler, Gene. *A Solo in Tom-Toms.* New York: Viking Press, 1946.

Frantz, Joe B., and Julian E. Choate, Jr. *The American Cowboy: The Myth and the Reality.* Norman: University of Oklahoma Press, 1955.

Hagedorn, Herman. *Roosevelt in the Badlands.* Boston: Houghton Mifflin, 1921.

Hassrick, Peter. *Frederic Remington.* Fort Worth, TX: The Amon Carter Museum of Western Art, 1973.

Havighurst, Walter. *Annie Oakley of the Wild West.* New York: Macmillan, 1954.

_____. *Buffalo Bill's Great Wild West Show.* New York: Random House, 1957.

Jarves, James Jackson. *The Art Idea,* ed. Benjamin Rowland, Jr. Cambridge, MA: Harvard University Press, 1960

Kopit, Arthur. *Indians.* New York: Hill and Wang, 1969.

Lamar, Howard R. (ed.). *Reader's Encyclopedia of the American West.* New York: Thomas Y. Crowell Company, 1977.

Mast, Gerald, and Marshall Cohen (eds.). *Film Theory and Criticism.* New York: Oxford University Press, 1979.

McCoy, Joseph G. *Historic Sketches of the Cattle Trade of the West and Southwest.* Kansas City, MO: Ramsey, Millett & Hudson, 1874.

McCracken. Harold, *Frederic Remington: Artist of the Old West.* Philadelphia: Lippincott, 1947.

Monaghan, Jay. *The Great Rascal.* Boston: Little, Brown and Company, 1952.

Murray, Marian. *Circus: From Rome to Ringling.* New York: Appleton-Century-Crofts, 1956.

Neihardt, John G. *Black Elk Speaks.* New York: William Morrow & Co., 1932.

Niver, Kemp R. *Motion Pictures from the Library of Congress Paper Print Collection 1894—1912.* Berkeley and Los Angeles: University of California Press, 1967.

Rennert, Jack. *100 Posters of Buffalo Bill's Wild West.* New York: Darien House, 1976.

Richardson, Albert D. *Beyond the Mississippi.* Hartford, CT: American Publishing, 1869.

Rogers, Will. *Autobiography,* ed. Donald Day. Boston: Houghton Mifflin, 1949.

Rollins, Philip Ashton. *The Cowboy, His Characteristics, His Equipment and His Part in the Development of the West.* New York: Charles Scribner's Sons, 1922.

Ross, Marvin C. *The West of Alfred Jacob Miller.* Norman: University of Oklahoma Press, 1968.

Rossi, Paul A., and David C. Hunt. *The Art of the Old West.* New York: Alfred A. Knopf, 1971.

Russell, Don. *The Lives and Legends of Buffalo Bill.* Norman: University of Oklahoma Press, 1960.

_____. *The Wild West: A History of Wild West Shows.* Fort Worth, TX: Amon Carter Museum of Western Art, 1961.

Sell, Henry Blackman, and Victor Weybright. *Buffalo Bill and the Wild West.* New York: Oxford University Press, 1955.

Sellers, Charles C. *The Artist of the Revolution: The Early Life of Charles Willson Peale.* Hebron, CT: Feather & Good, 1939.

Siringo, Charles A. *A Texas Cowboy.* Lincoln: University of Nebraska Press, 1966.

Slotkin, Richard. *Regeneration Through Violence: The Mythology of the American Frontier 1600—1860.* Middletown, CT: Wesleyan University Press, 1973.

Smith, Henry Nash. *Virgin Land: The American West as Symbol and Myth.* Cambridge, MA: Harvard University Press, 1950.

Standing Bear, Luther. *My People the Sioux,* ed. E. A. Brininstool. Boston: Houghton Mifflin, 1928.

Stanley, John Mix. *Scenes and Incidents of Stanley's Western Wilds.* Washington, DC: 1854.

Streeter, Floyd B. *Prairie Trails and Cow Towns.* Boston: Chapman & Grimes, 1936.

Talbot, Daniel (ed.). *Film: An Anthology.* Berkeley and Los Angeles: University of California Press, 1967.

Vestal, Stanley. *Sitting Bull: Champion of the Sioux.* Boston: Houghton Mifflin, 1932

Walsh, Richard J. *The Making of Buffalo Bill.* New York: Bobbs-Merrill Co., 1928.

Ward, Fay. *The Cowboy at Work.* New York: Hastings House, 1958.

Webb, Walter Prescott. *The Great Plains.* New York: Grosset and Dunlap, 1931.

Wetmore, Helen Cody, and Zane Grey. *Last of the Great Scouts (Buffalo Bill).* New York: Grosset and Dunlap, 1918.

White, George Edward. *The Eastern Establishment and the Western Experience: The West of Frederic Remington, Theodore Roosevelt and Owen Wister.* New Haven, CT: Yale University Press, 1968.

Wister, Fanny Kemble. *Owen Wister Out West: His Journals and Letters.* Chicago: University of Chicago Press, 1958.